VINTAGE FACES
by CraftAndCherish

First Edition

ISBN: 979-8-30410-373-2

Publisher Information:
SNK Publishing, Published in collaboration with CraftAndCherish
Printed and distributed by: Amazon KDP

Disclaimer:
This book has been created with care to inspire creativity. The publisher and author accept no liability for how the materials are used beyond the intended purpose.

For permissions or inquiries, please contact: CraftAndCherish
https://craftandcherish.com/contact

A NOTE TO OUR READERS

Our books are printed and distributed by Amazon using various manufacturing facilities worldwide. While Amazon ensures quality, occasional issues such as faint printing, off-center text, or unusual odors may arise due to these variations.

If you encounter any such problems, we encourage you to contact Amazon's customer service for a replacement or refund. You can reach them at https://www.amazon.com/gp/help/customer/contact-us

Additionally, please note that some techniques, such as Gelli printing, may not perform optimally on certain paper types used in this book. This is a result of printing processes and materials. If you are unsatisfied, Amazon's customer service is ready to assist with your concerns.

If your concerns are not fully resolved or if you have any other questions, please feel free to reach out to us directly at contact@craftandcherish.com or via https://craftandcherish.com/contact

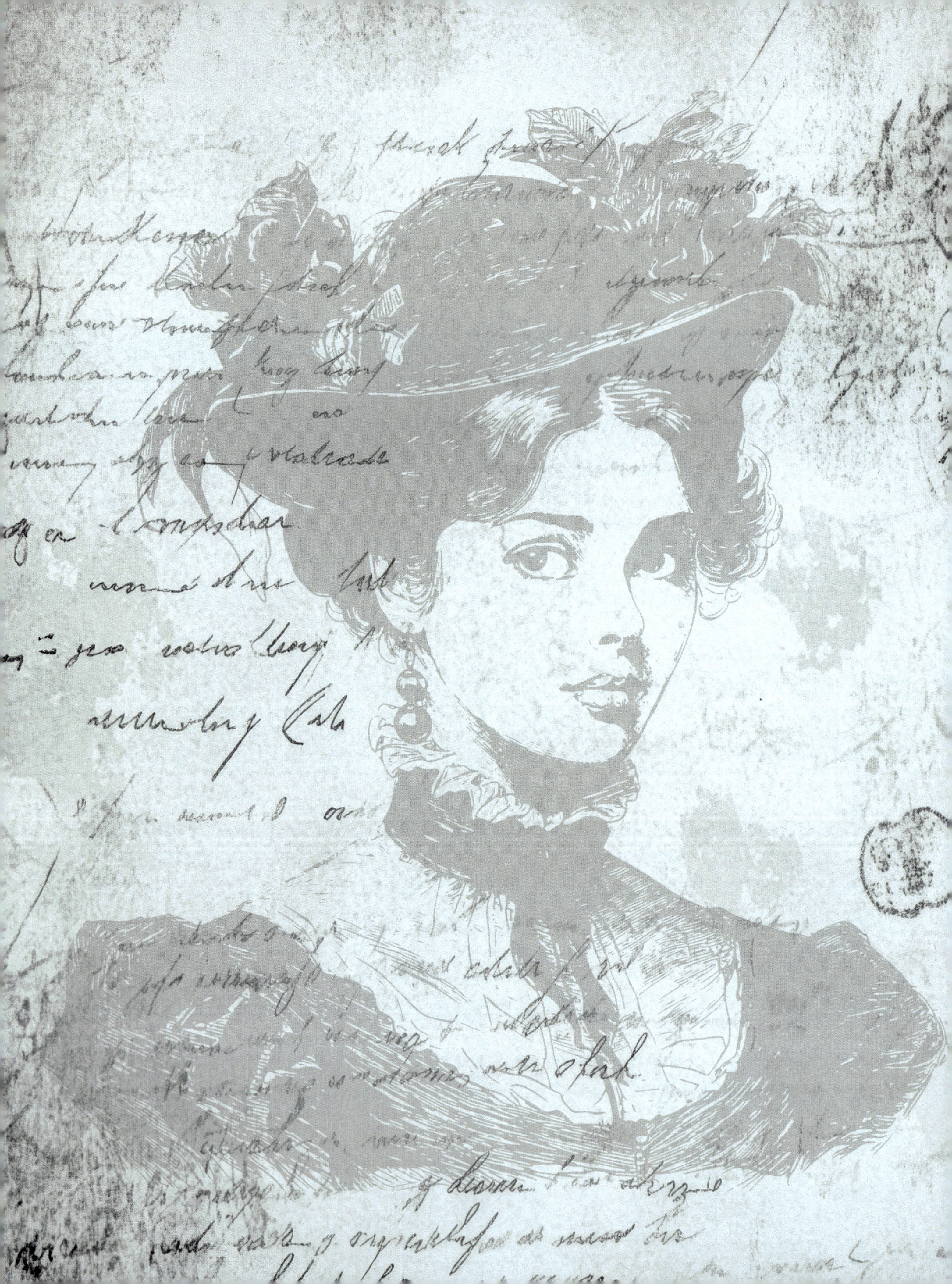

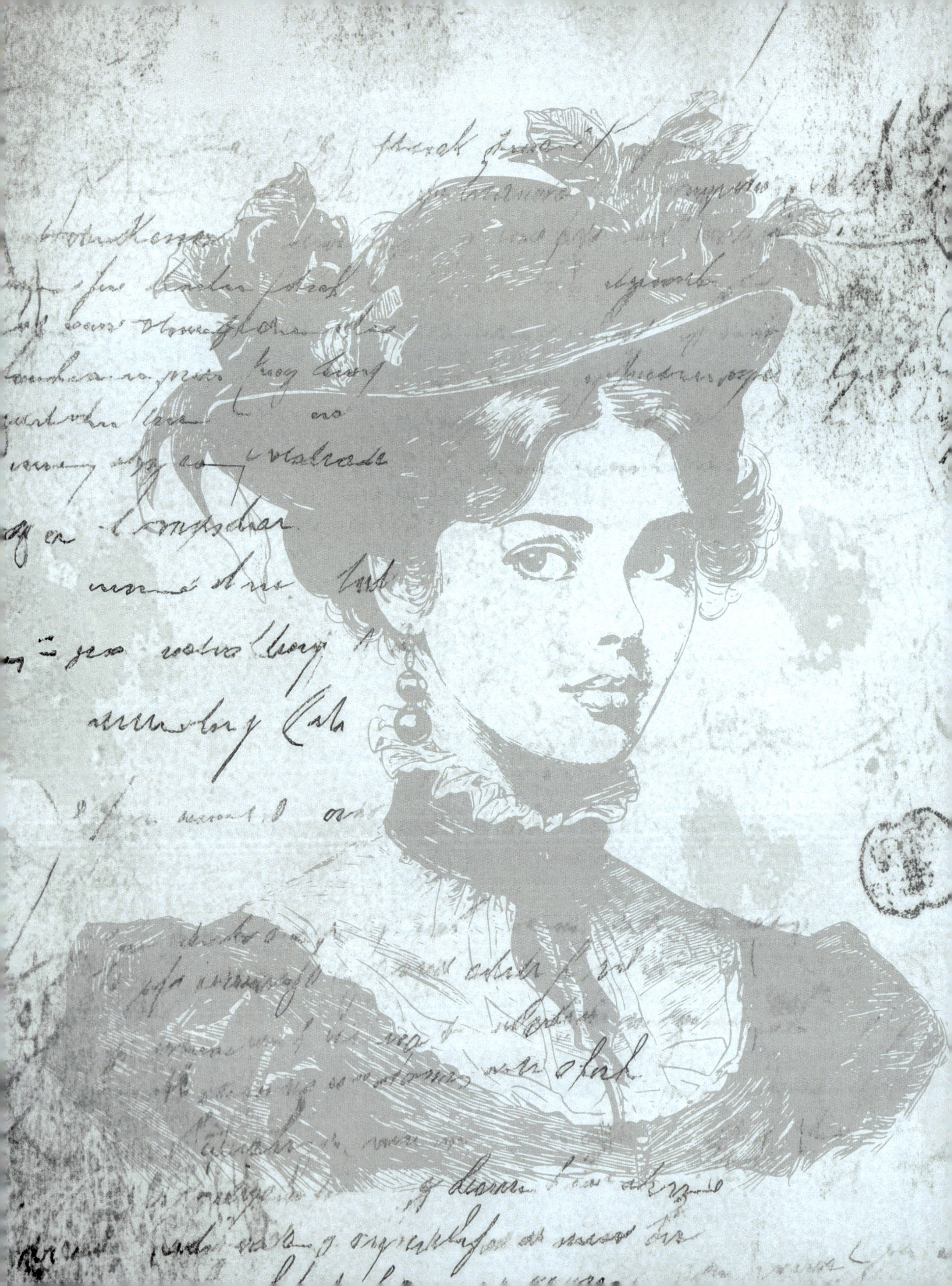

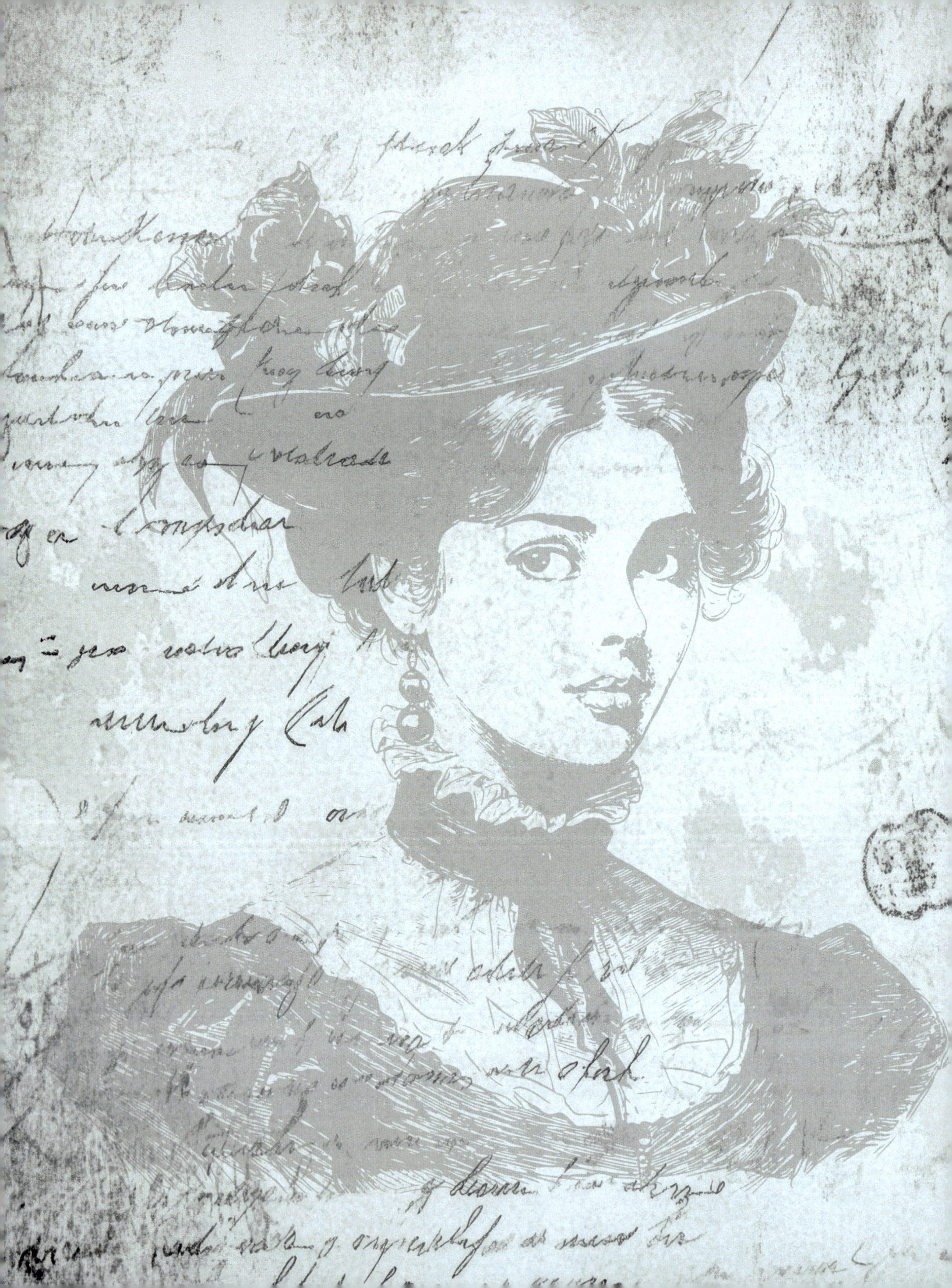

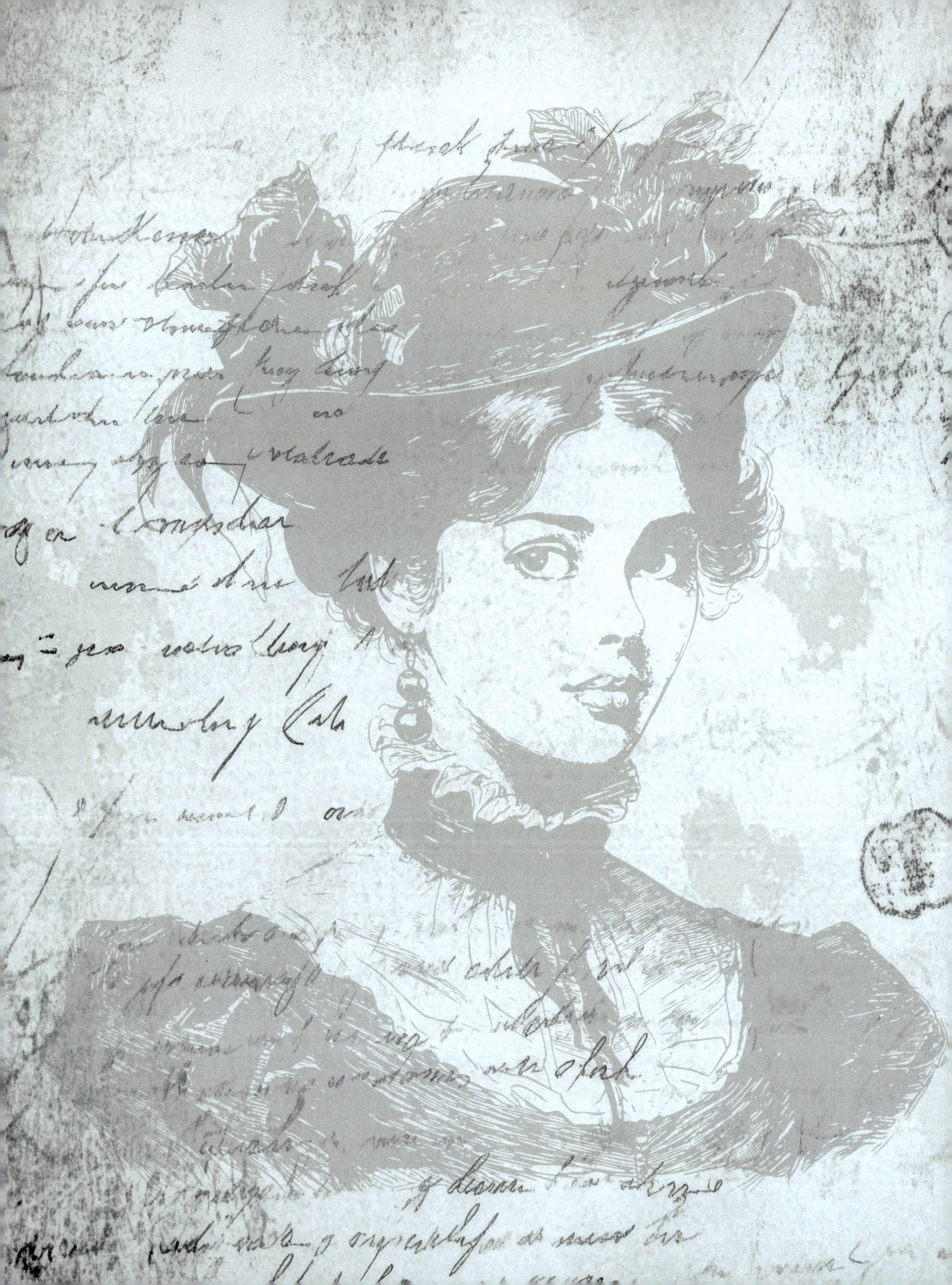

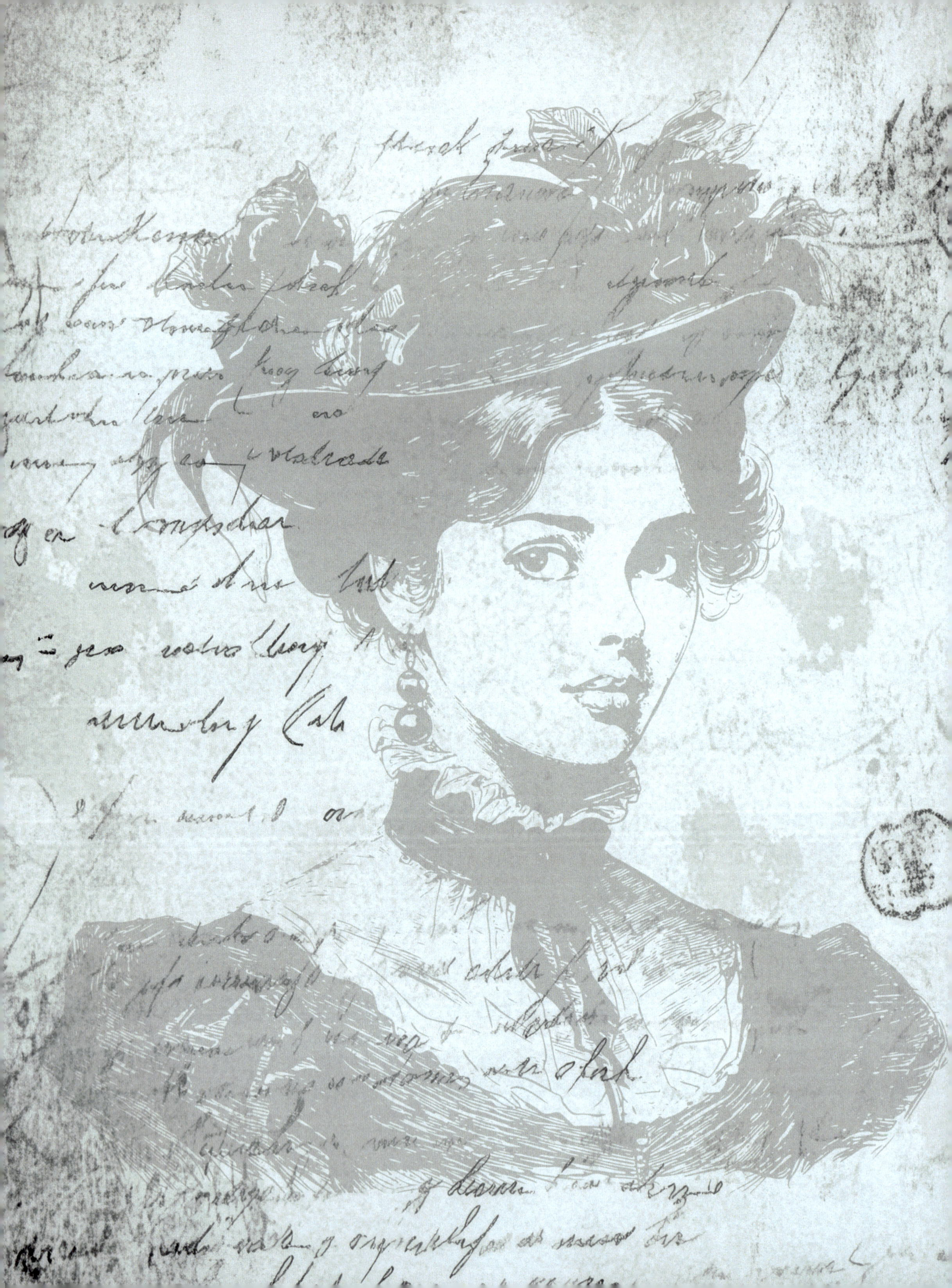

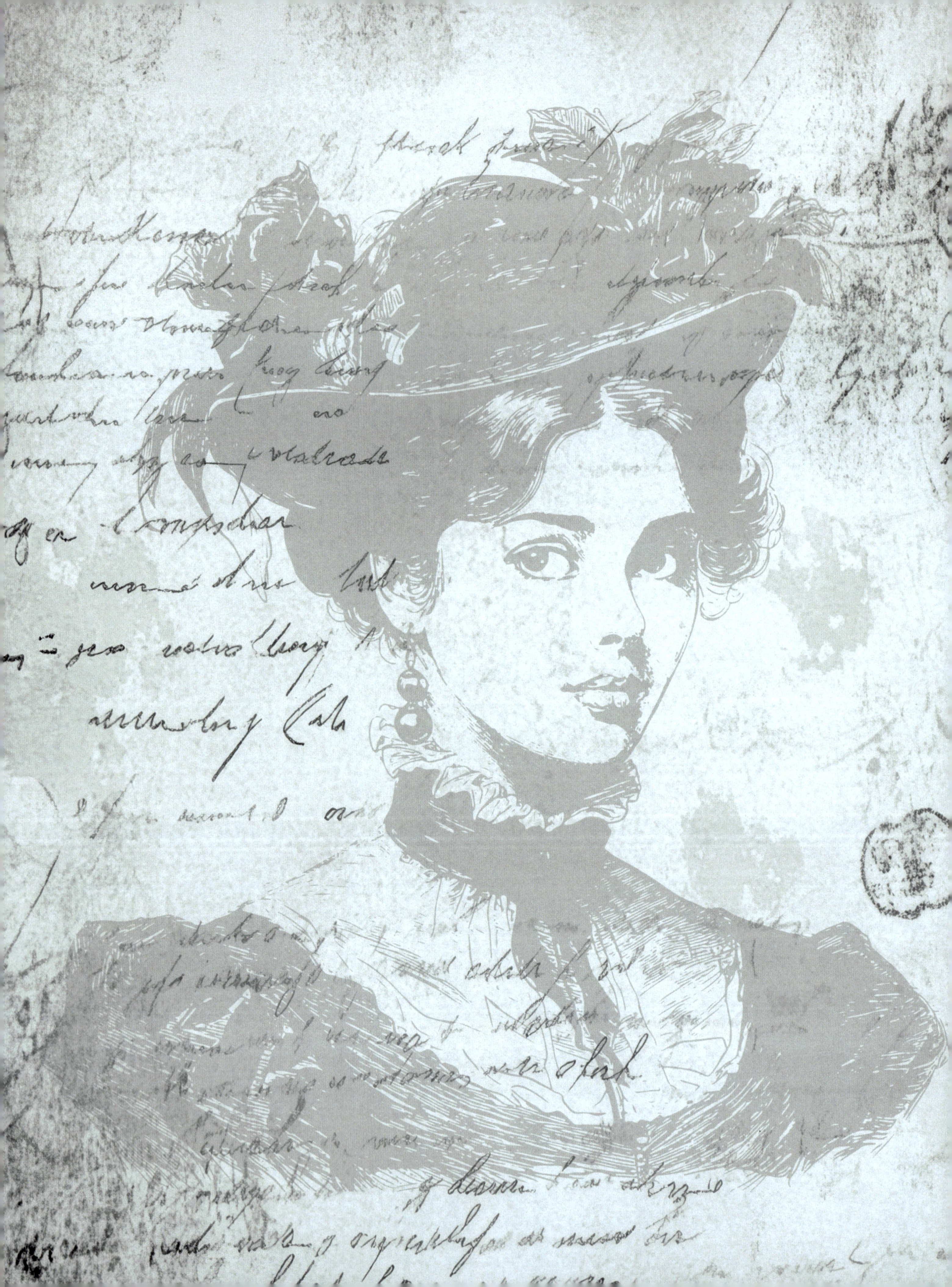

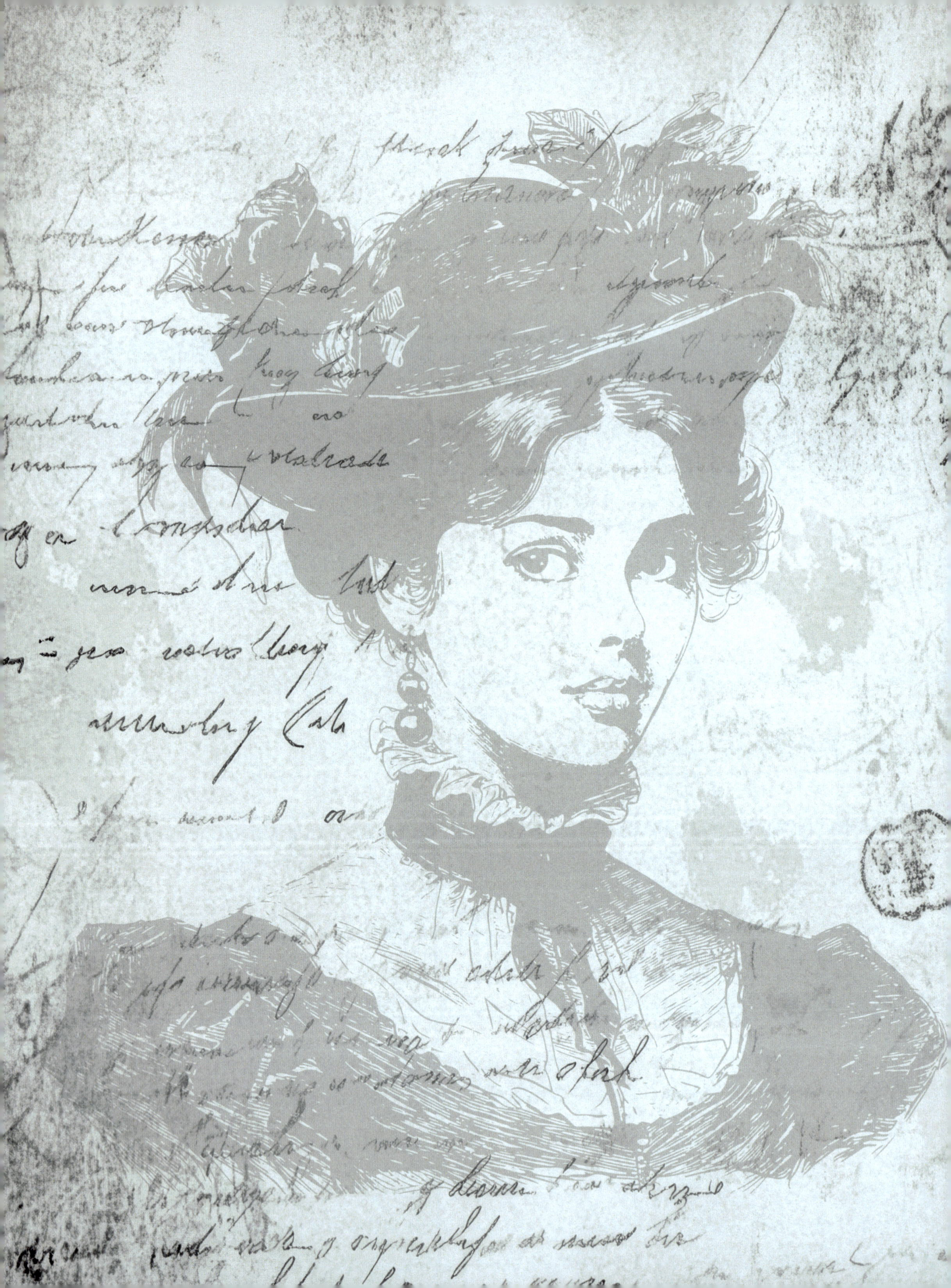

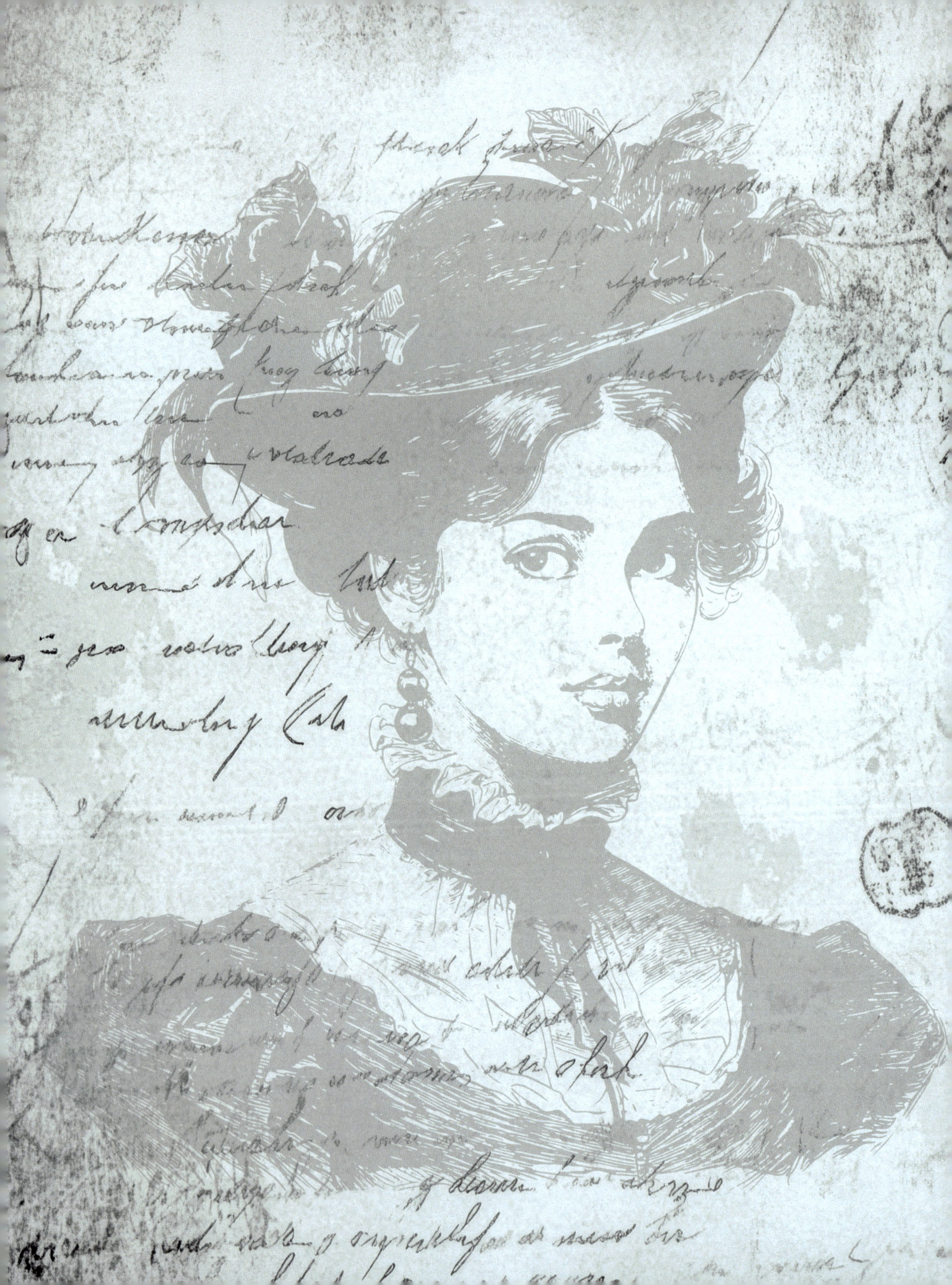

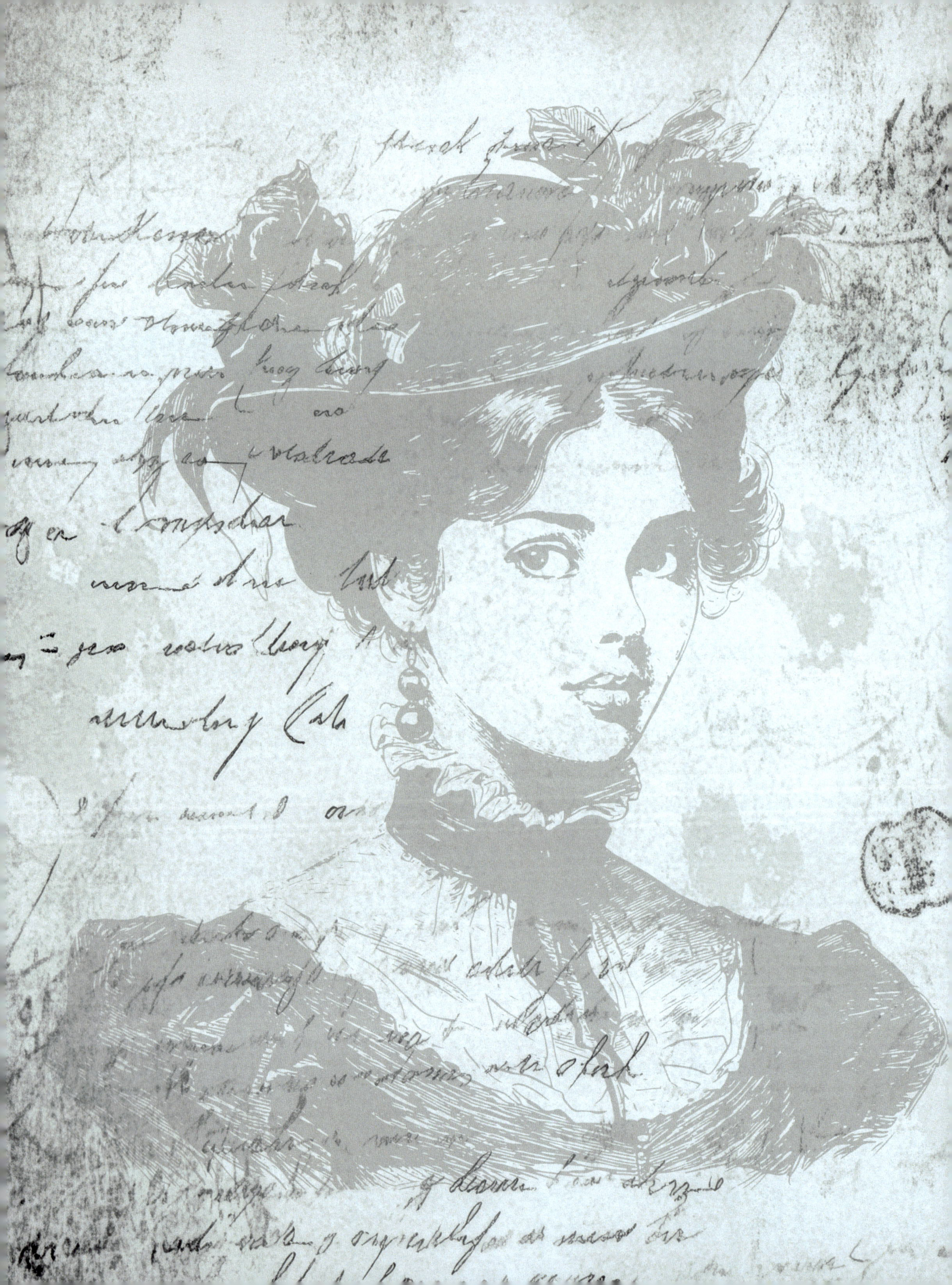

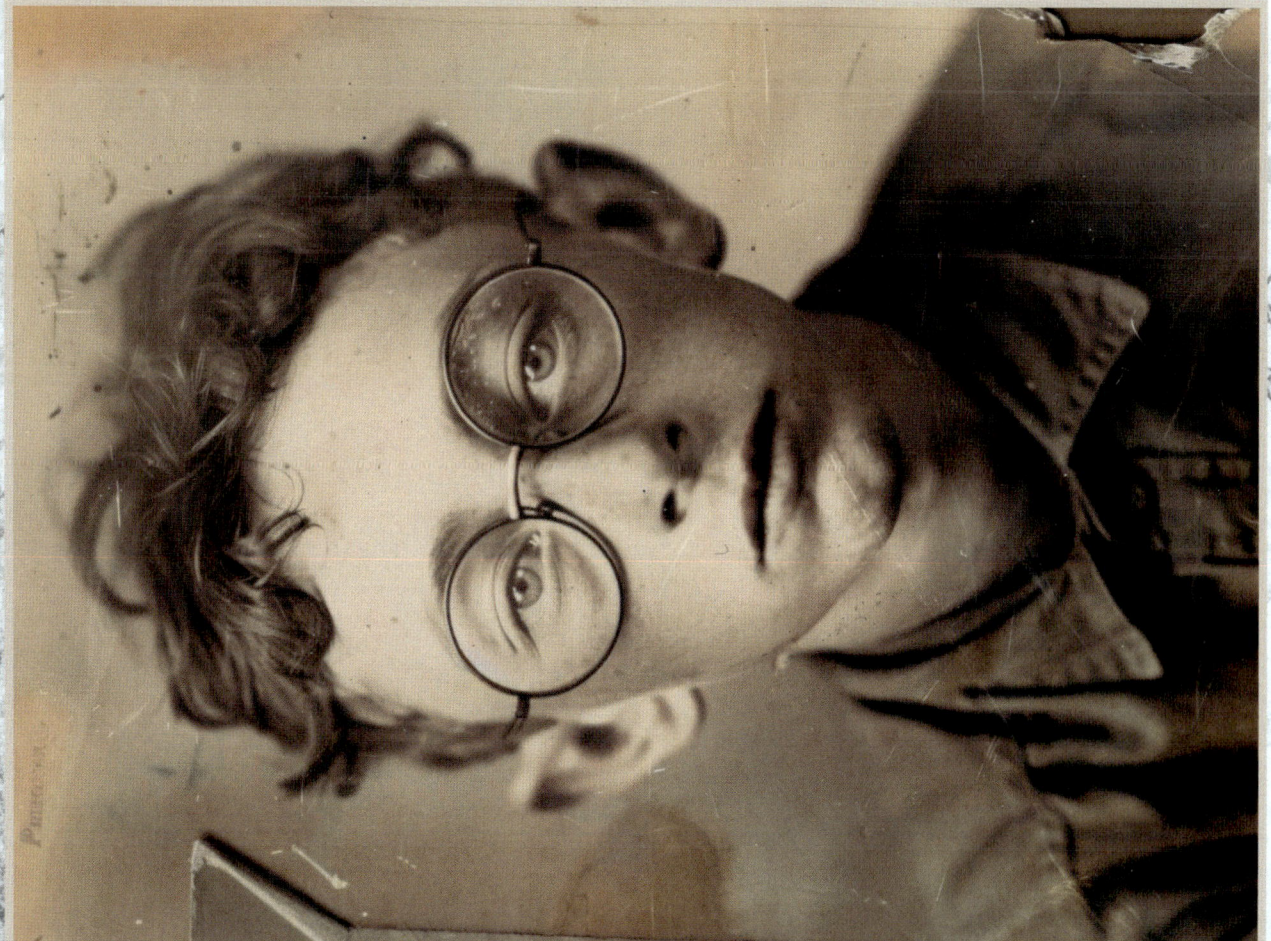

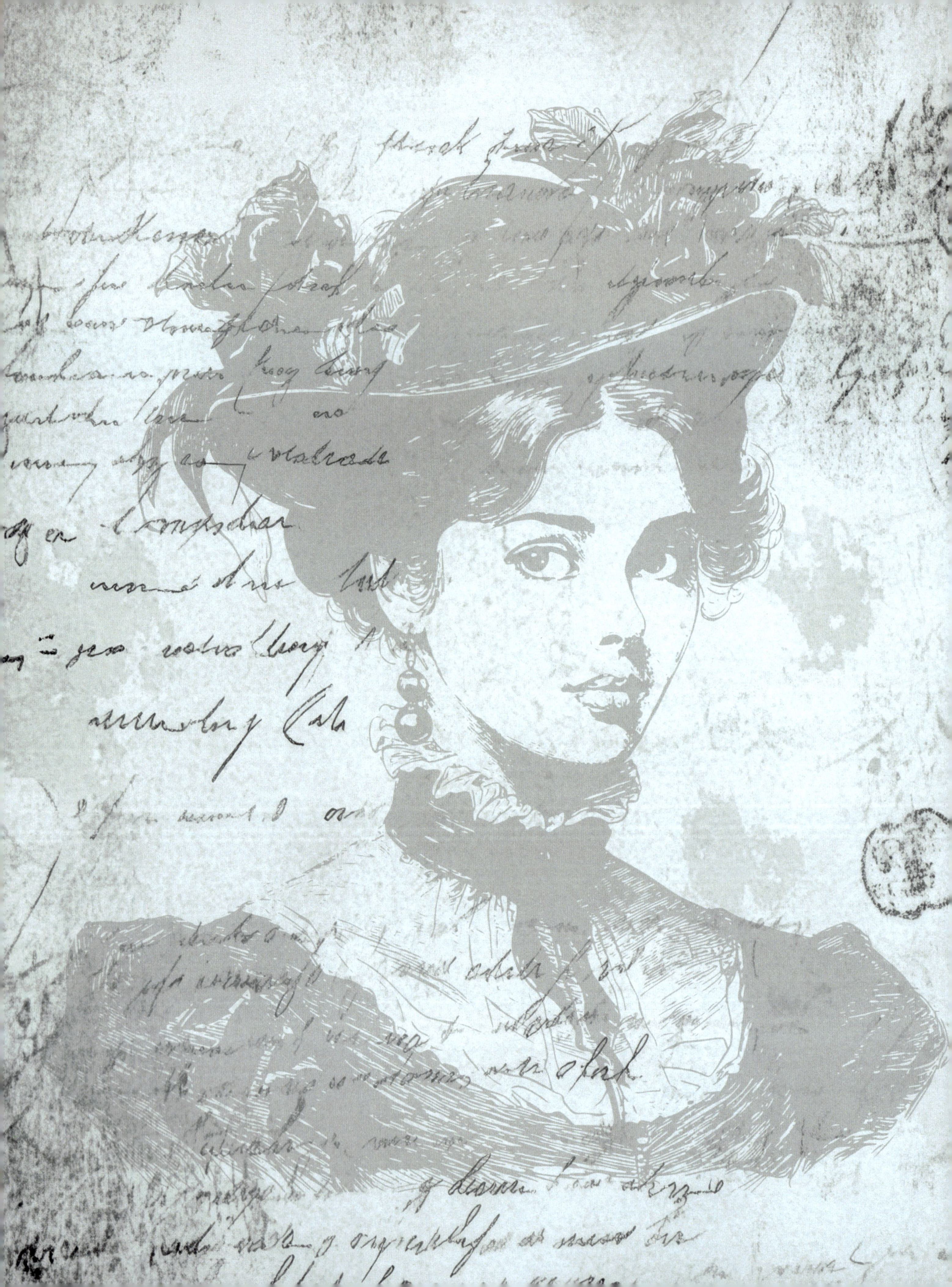

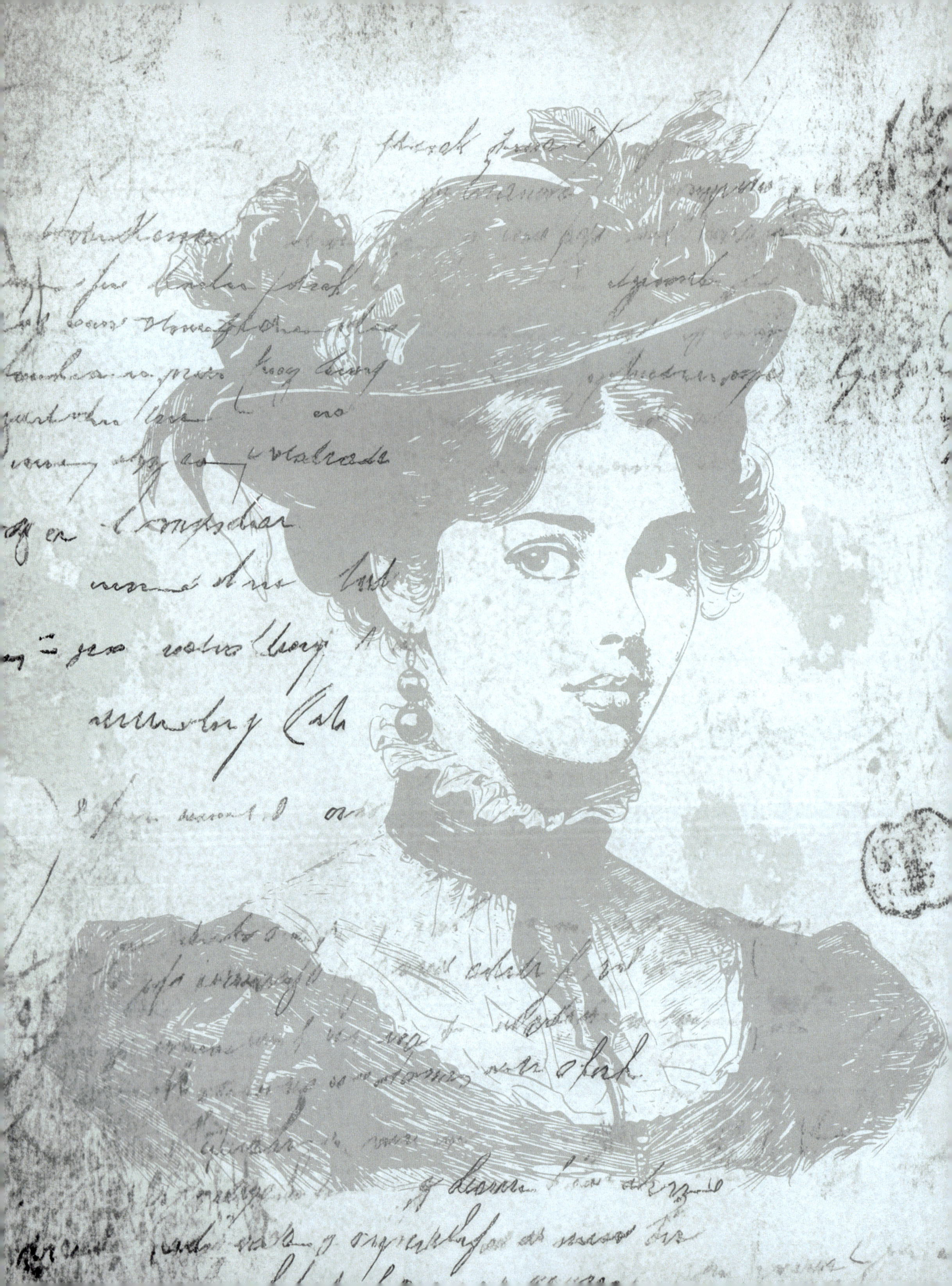

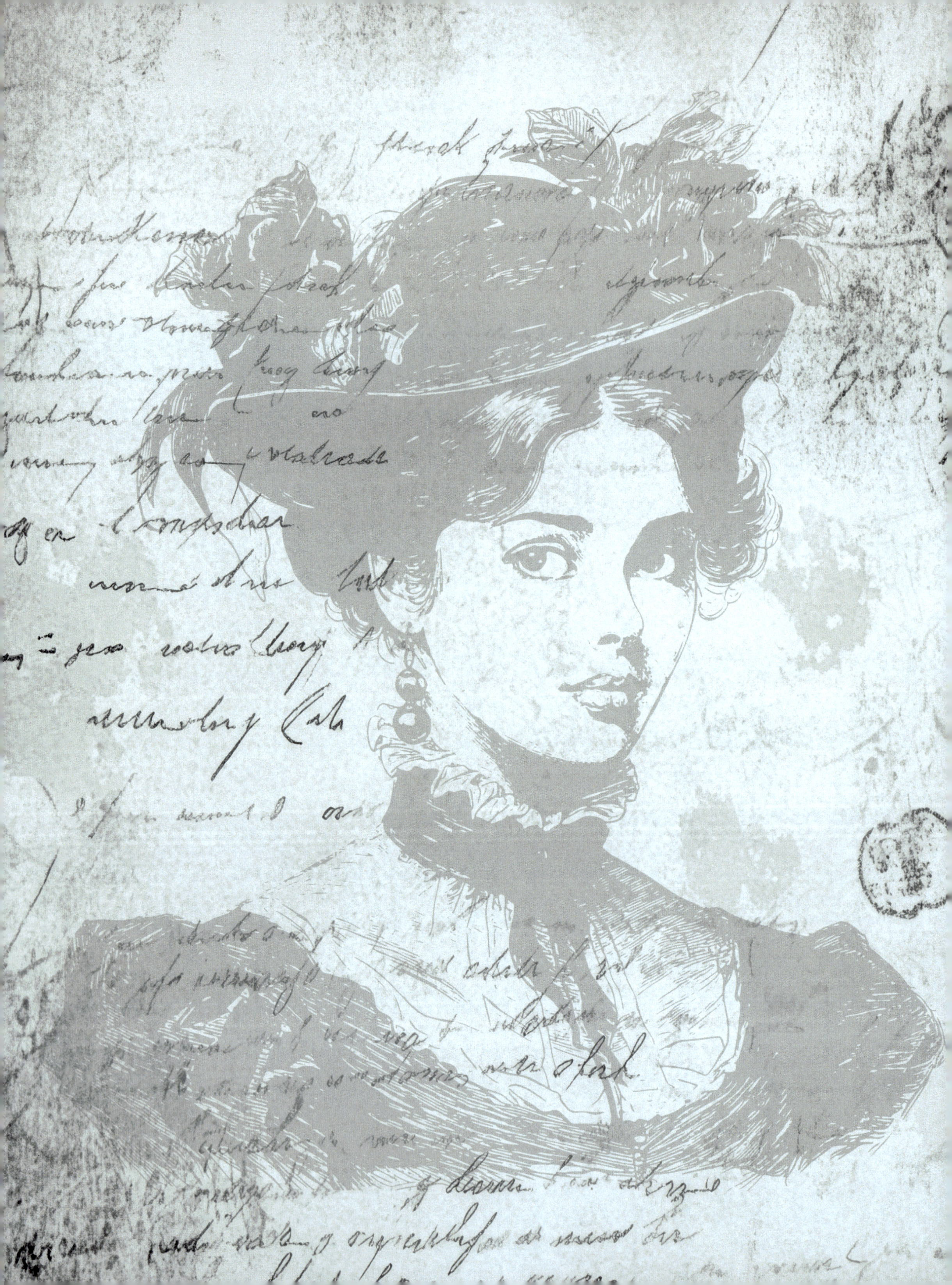

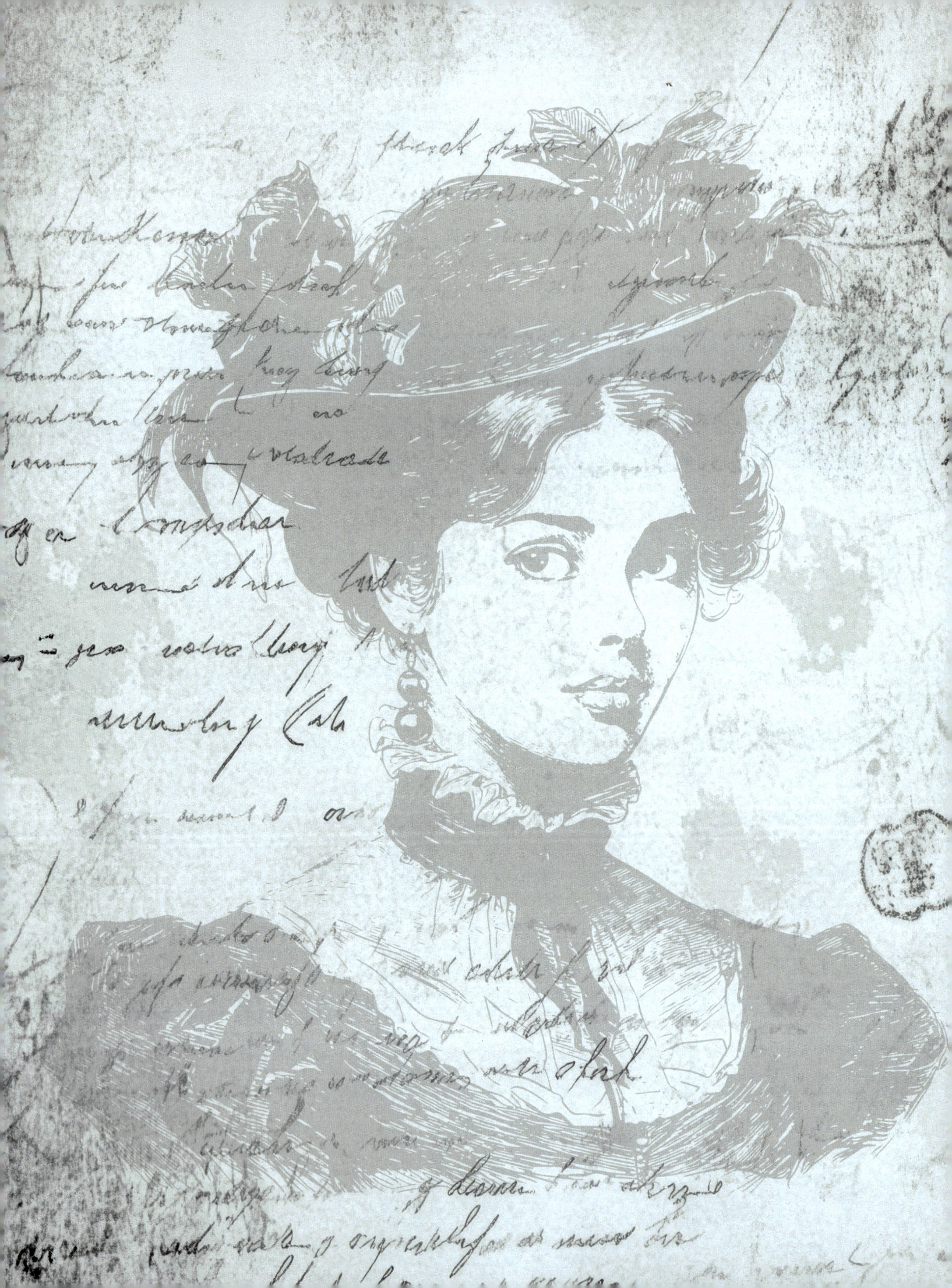

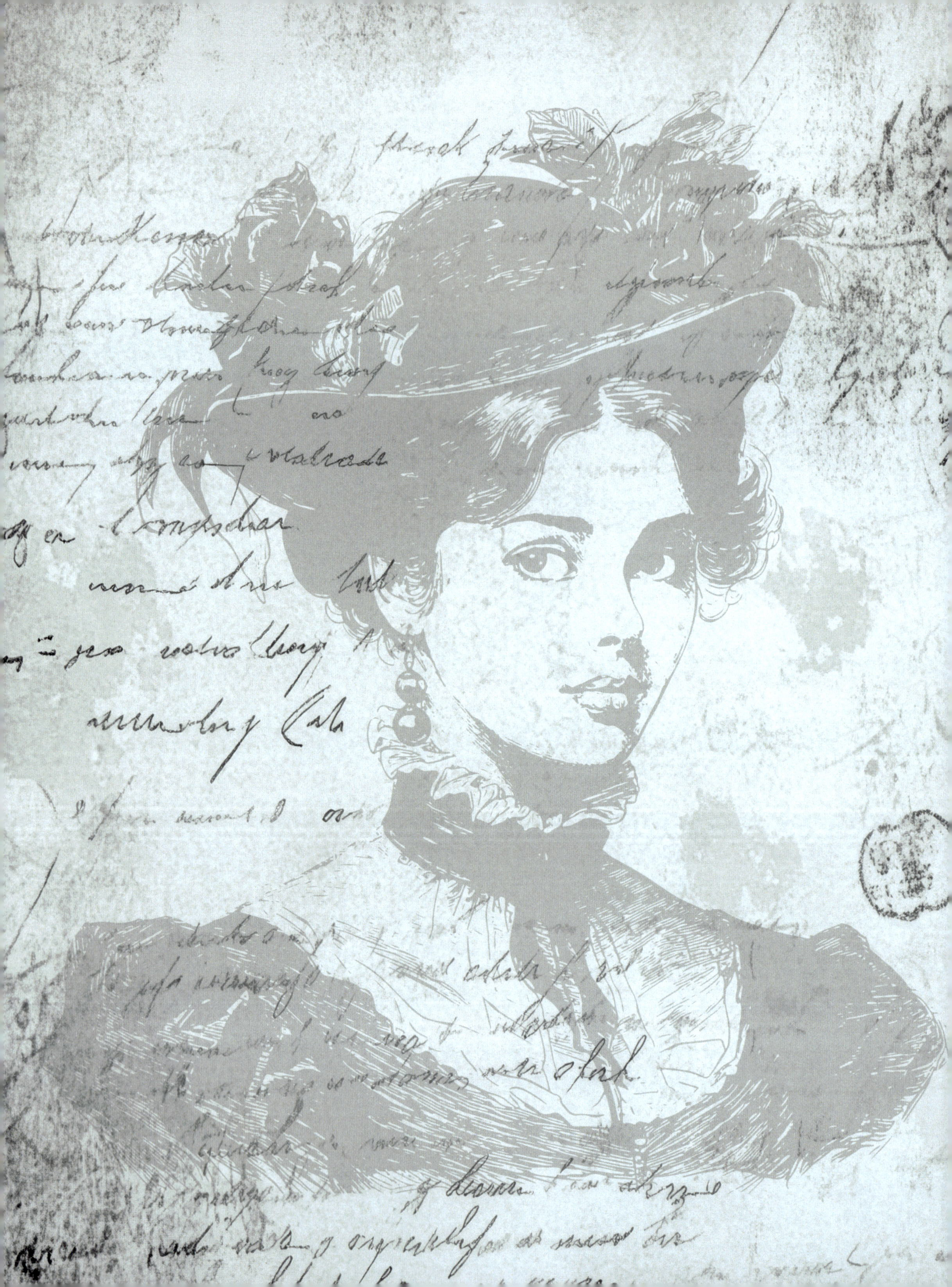

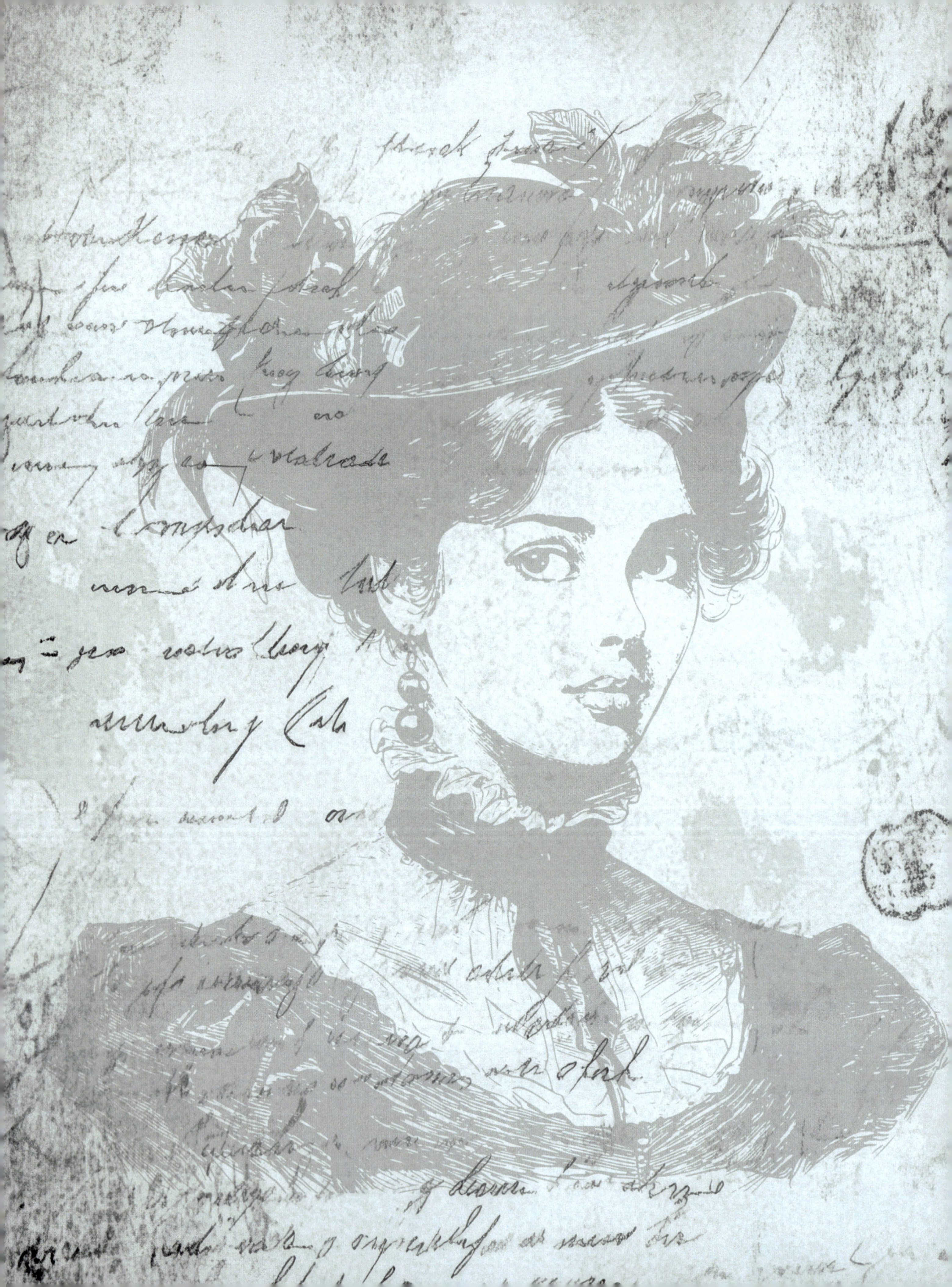

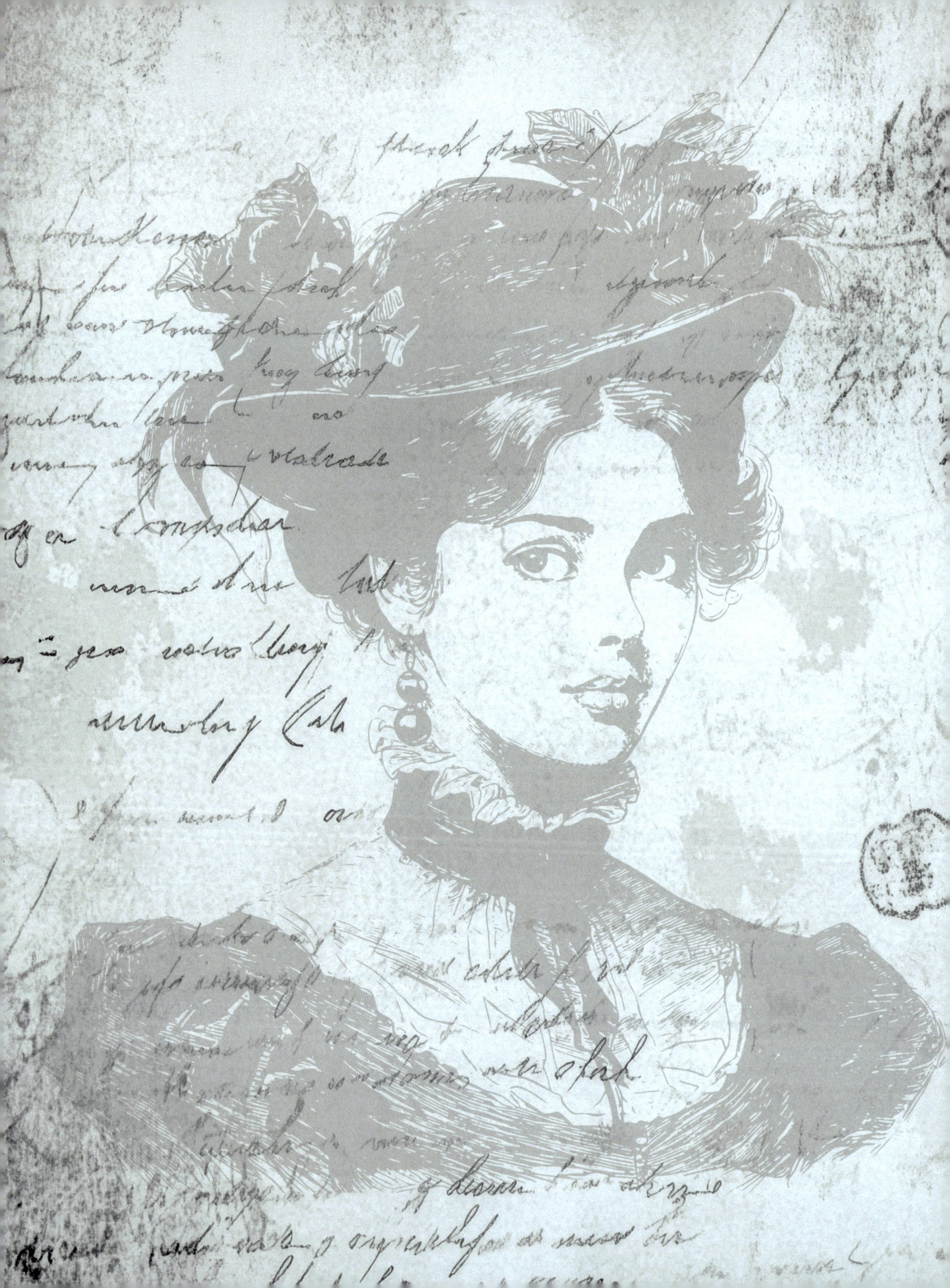

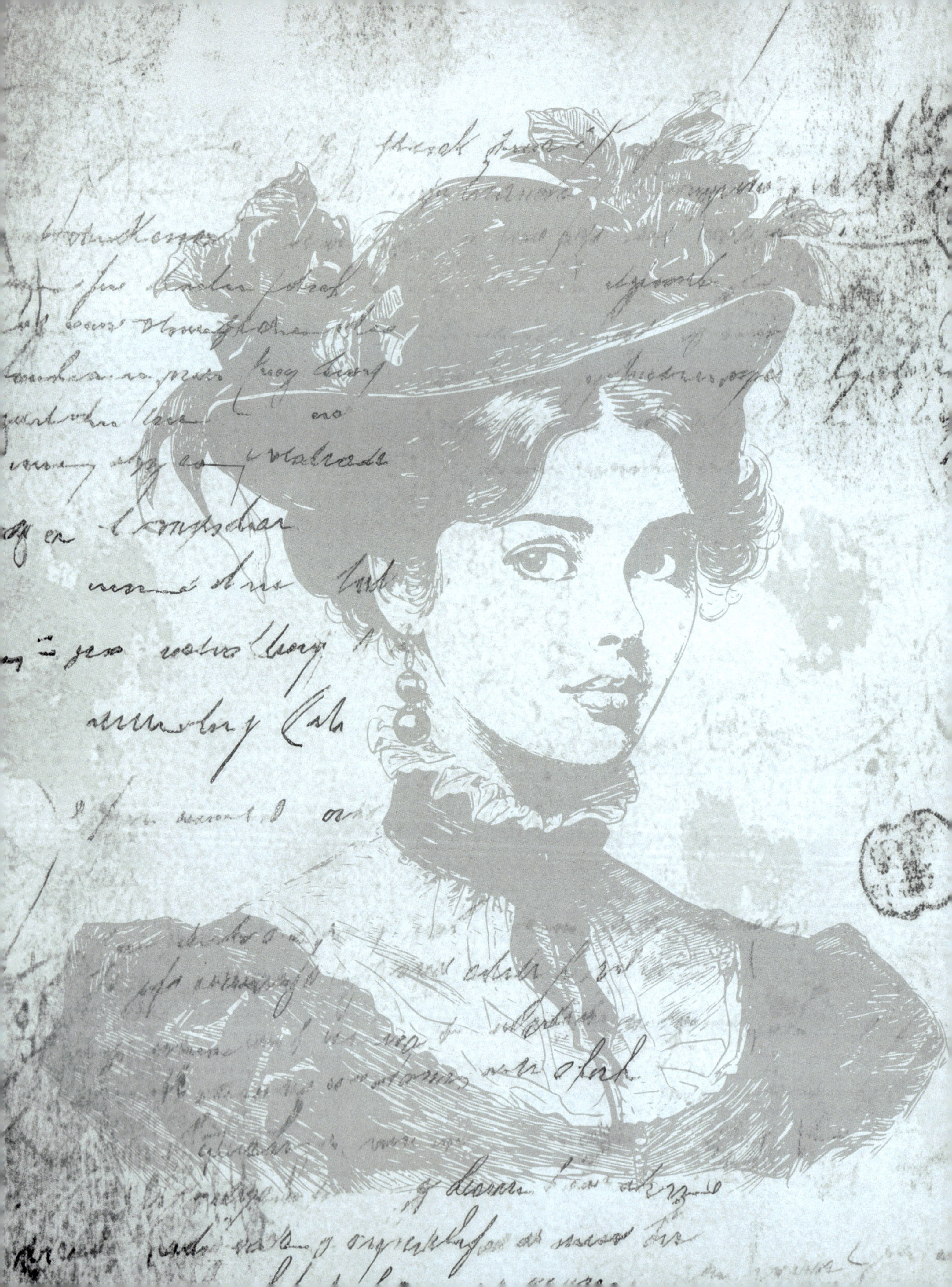

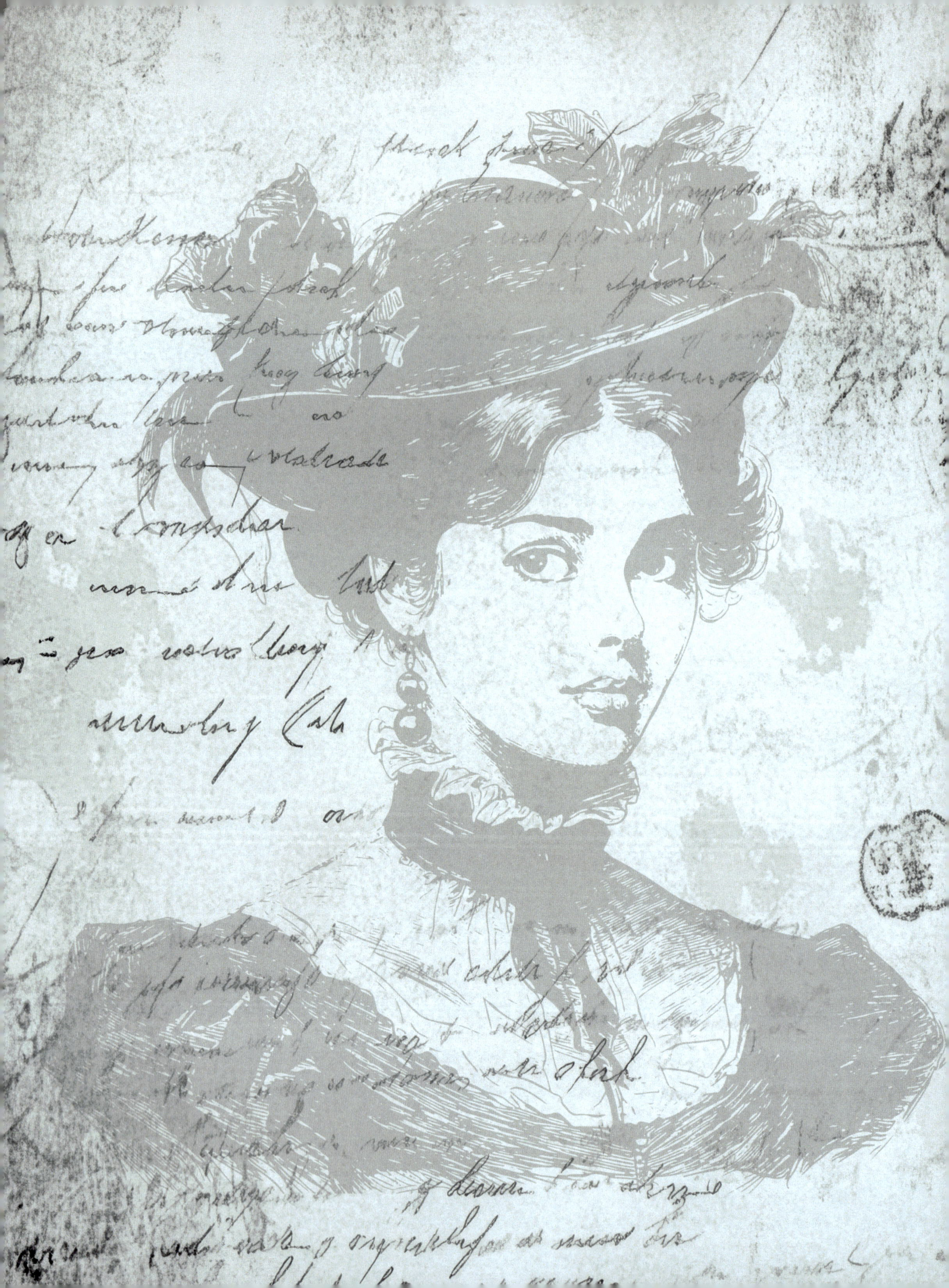

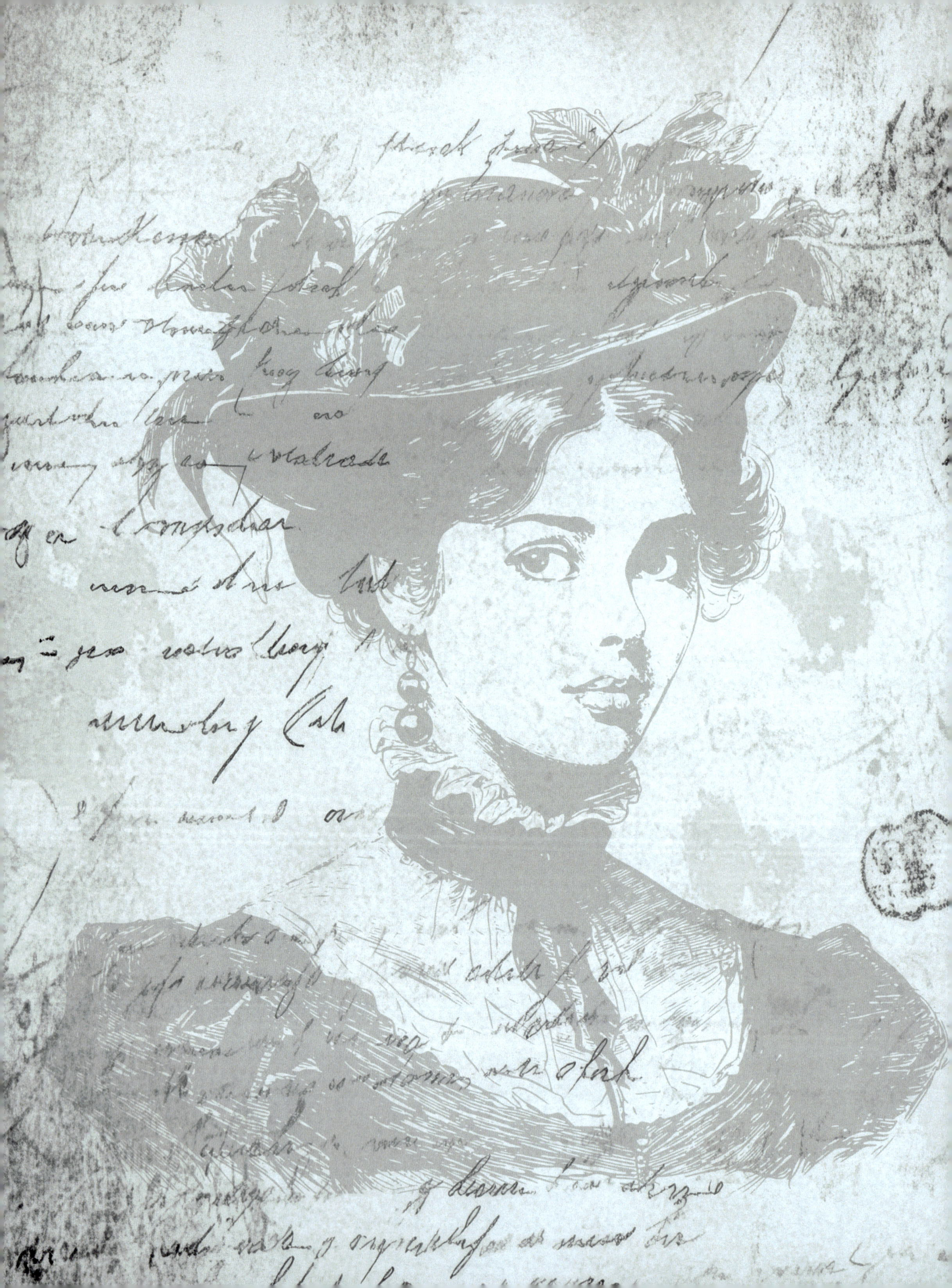

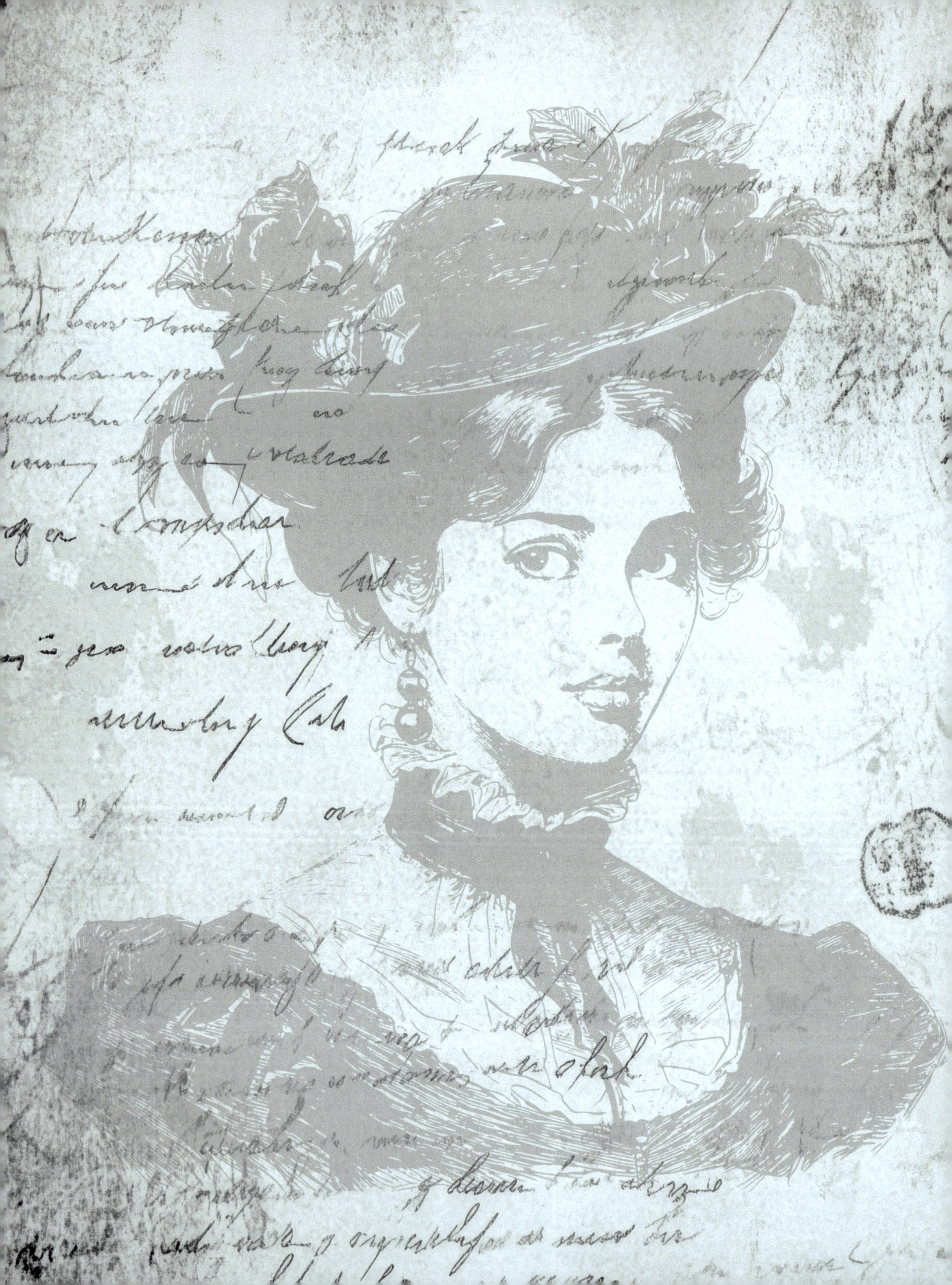

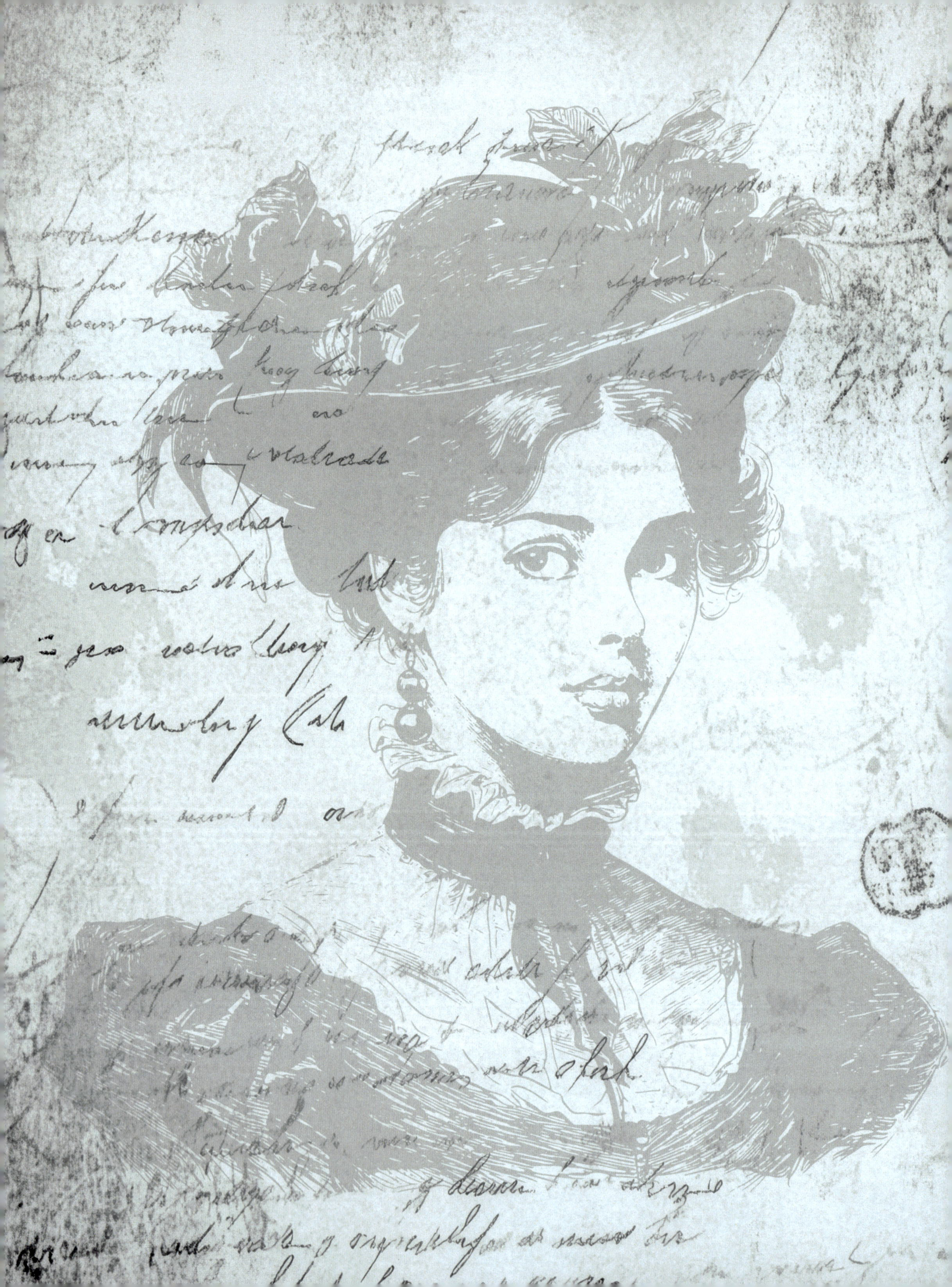

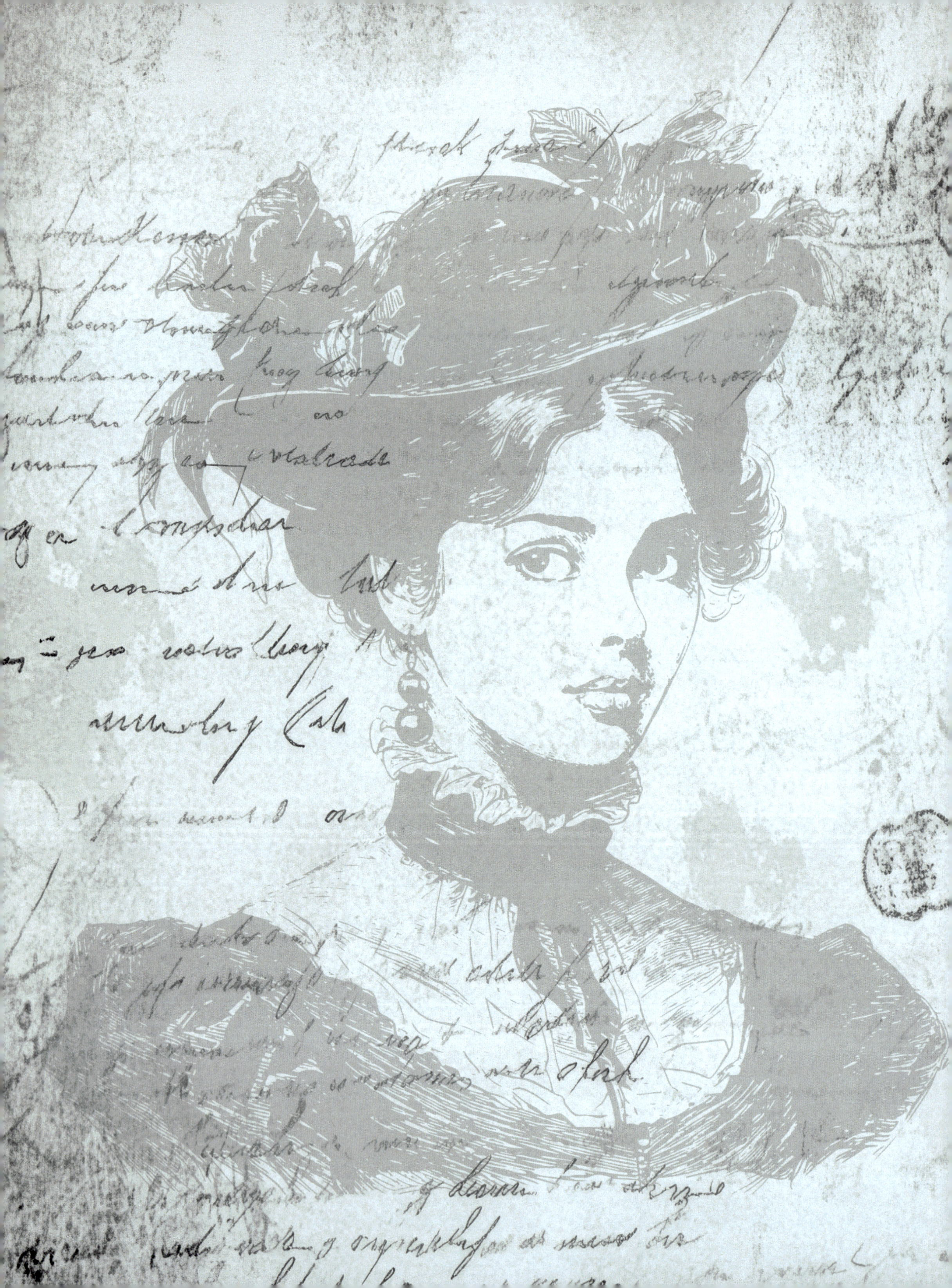

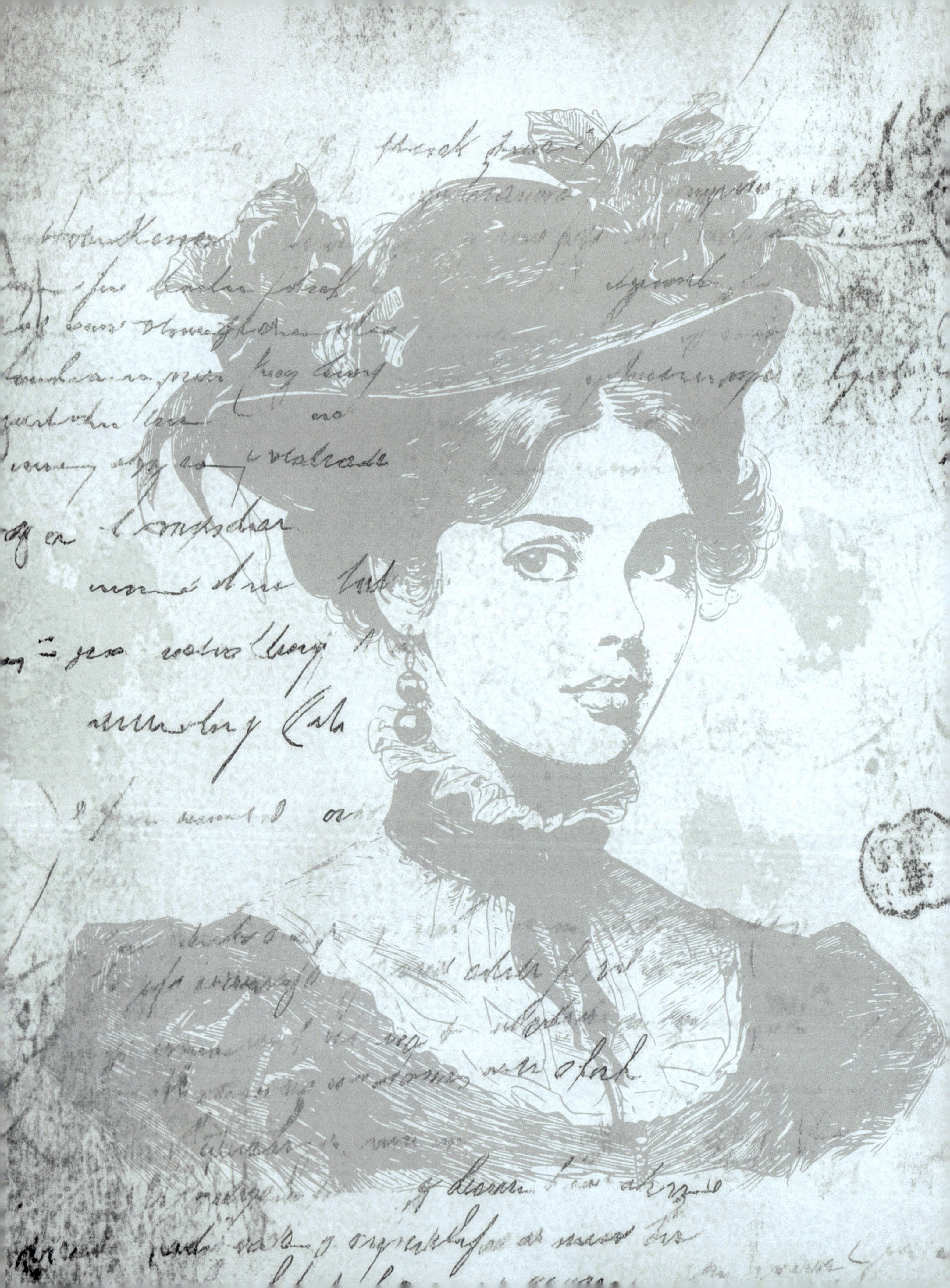

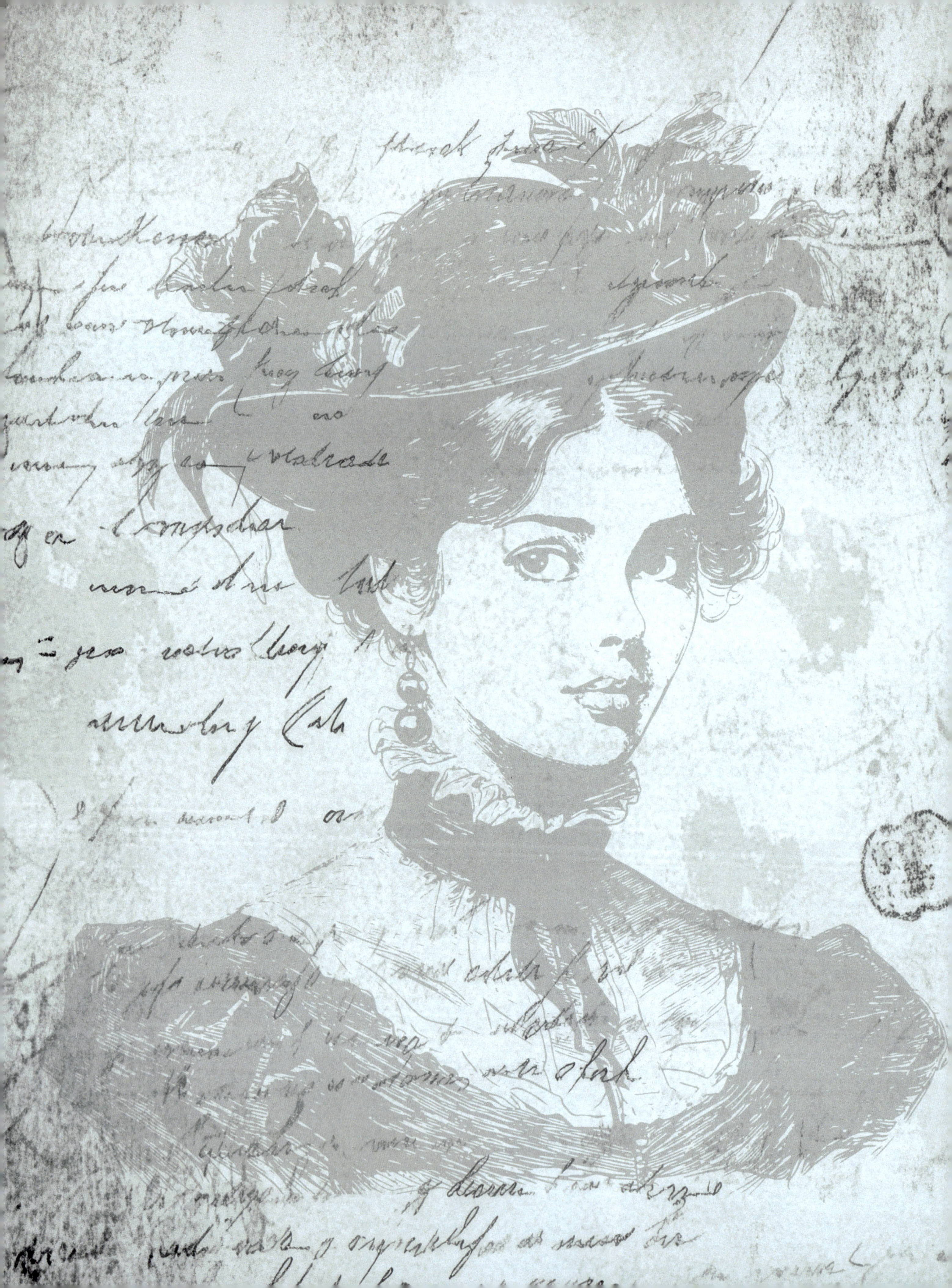

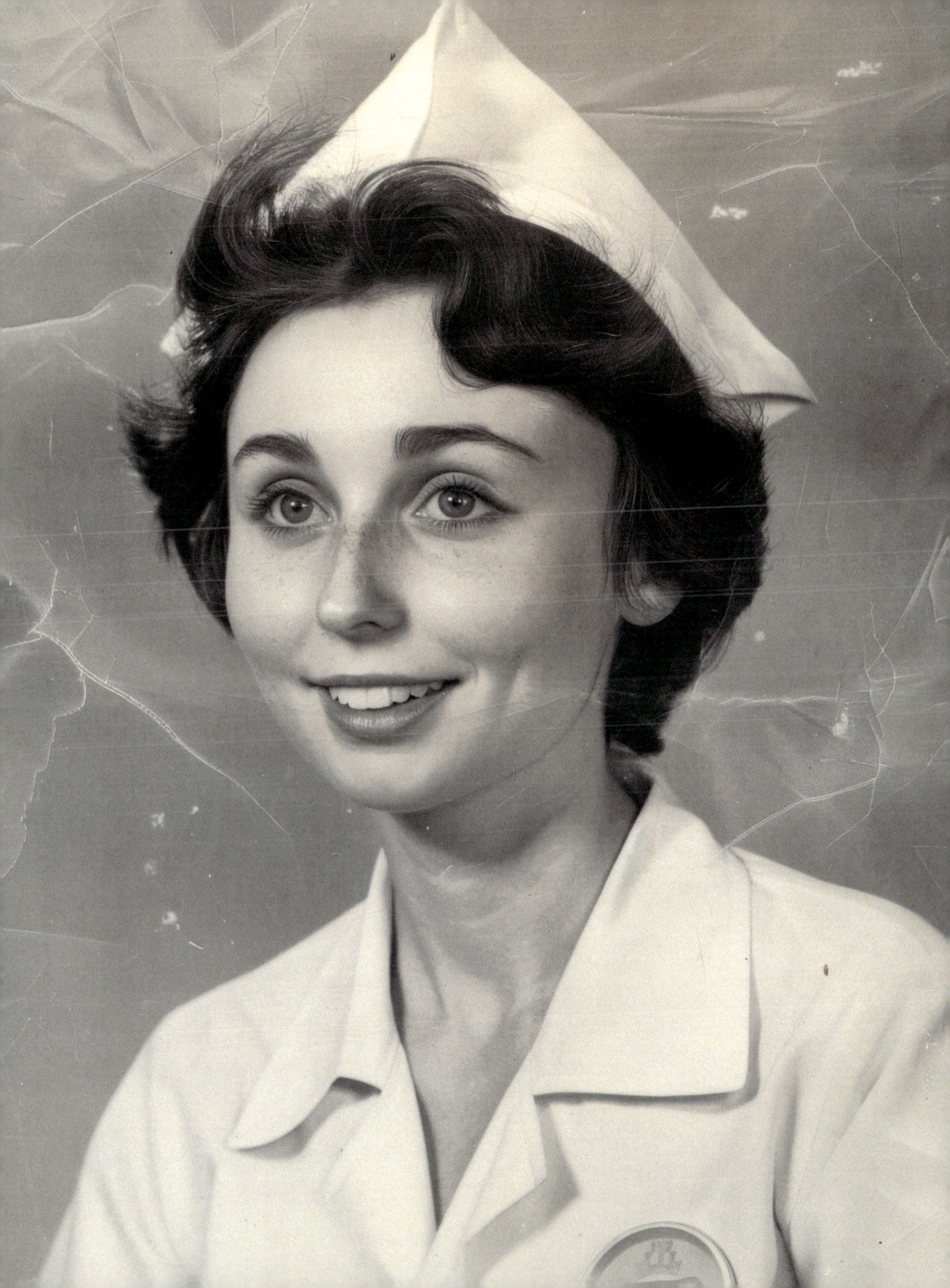

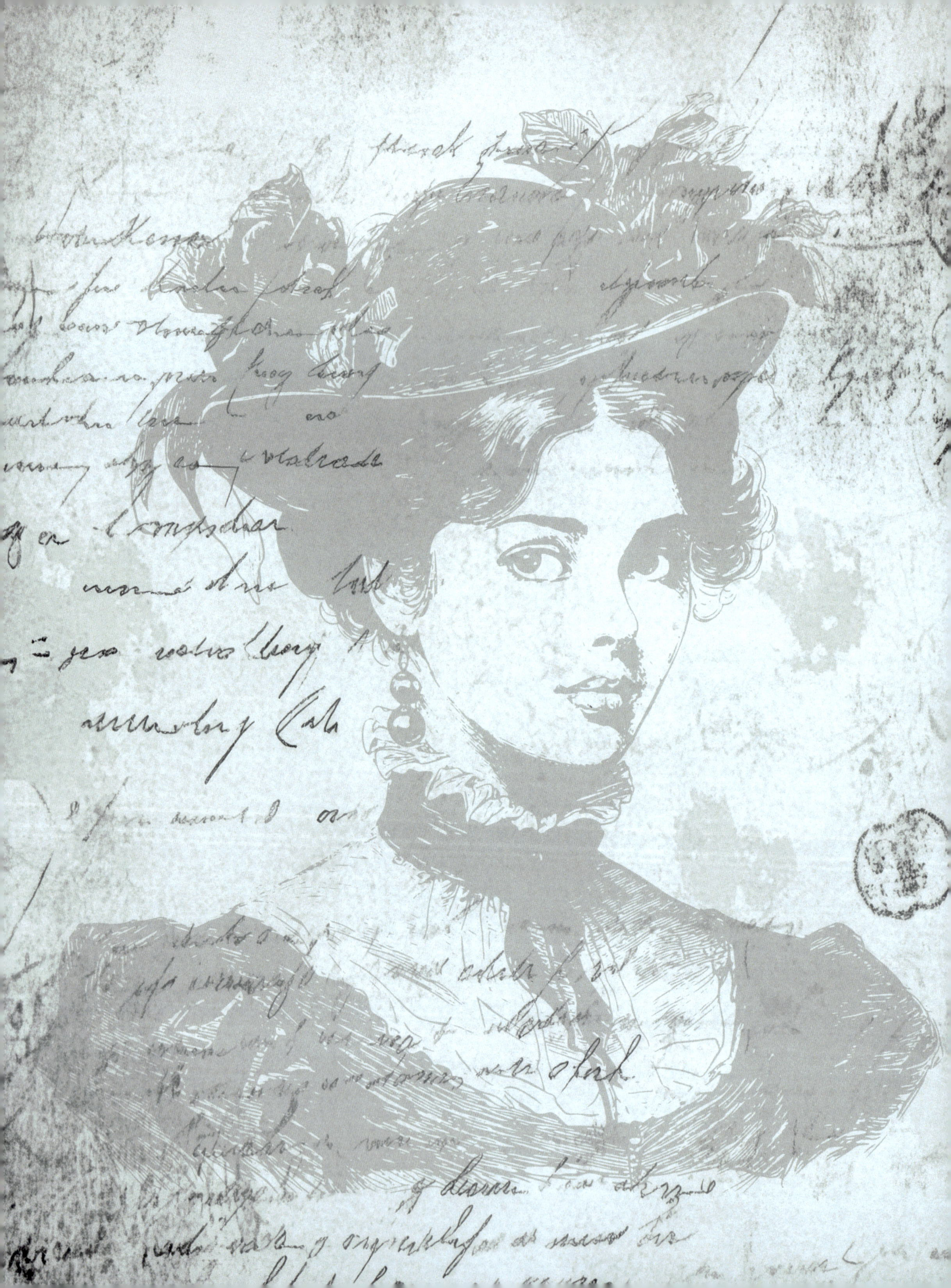

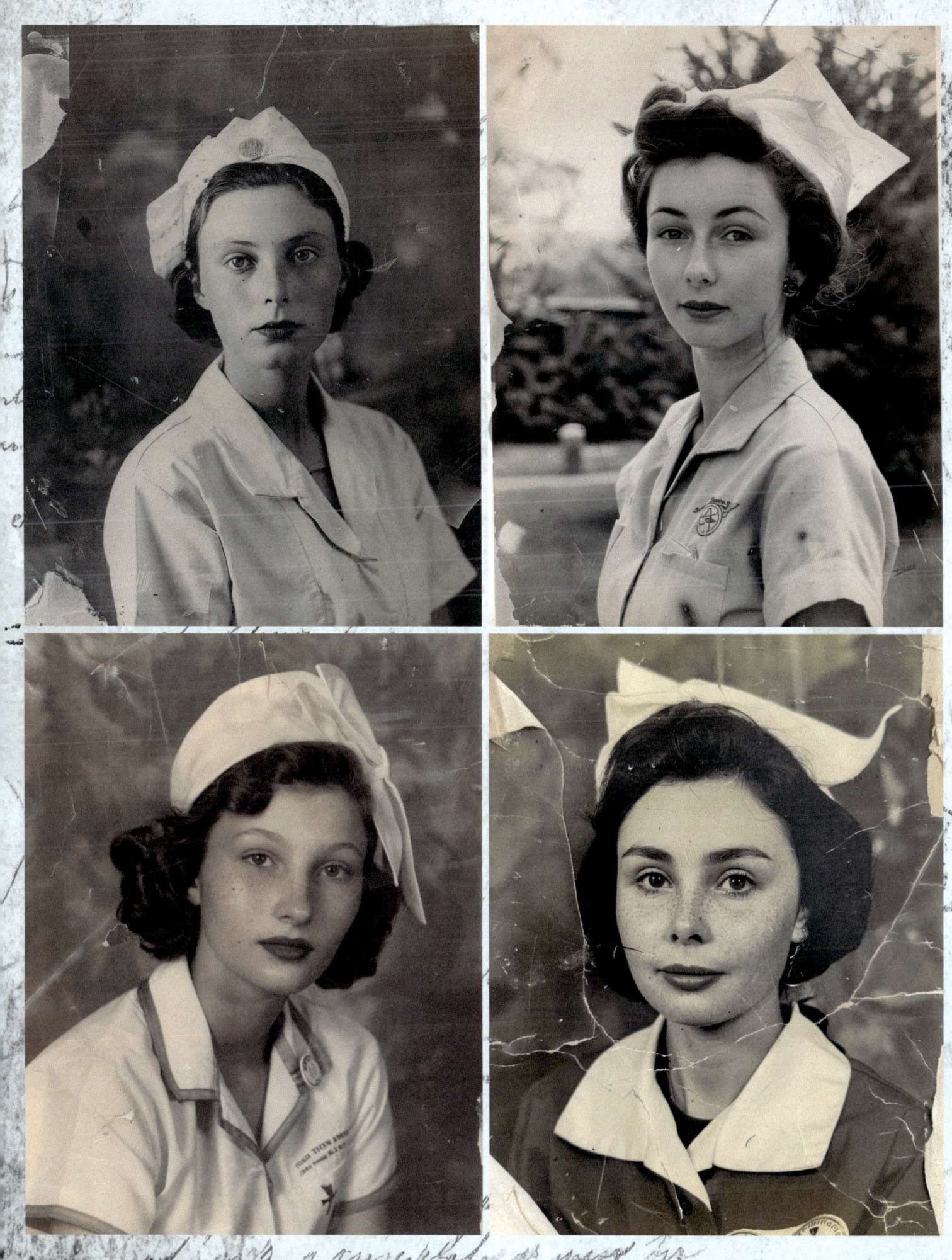

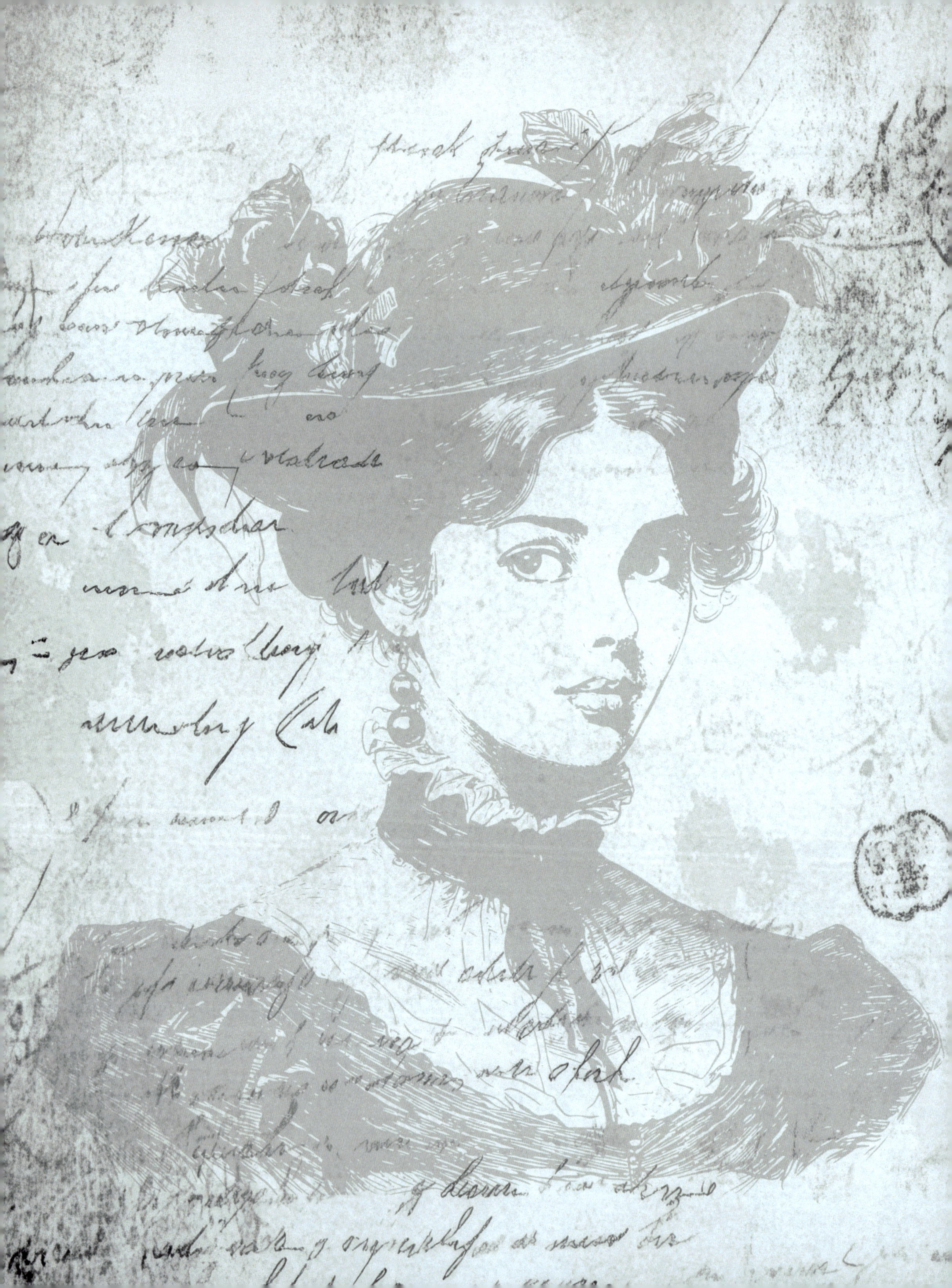

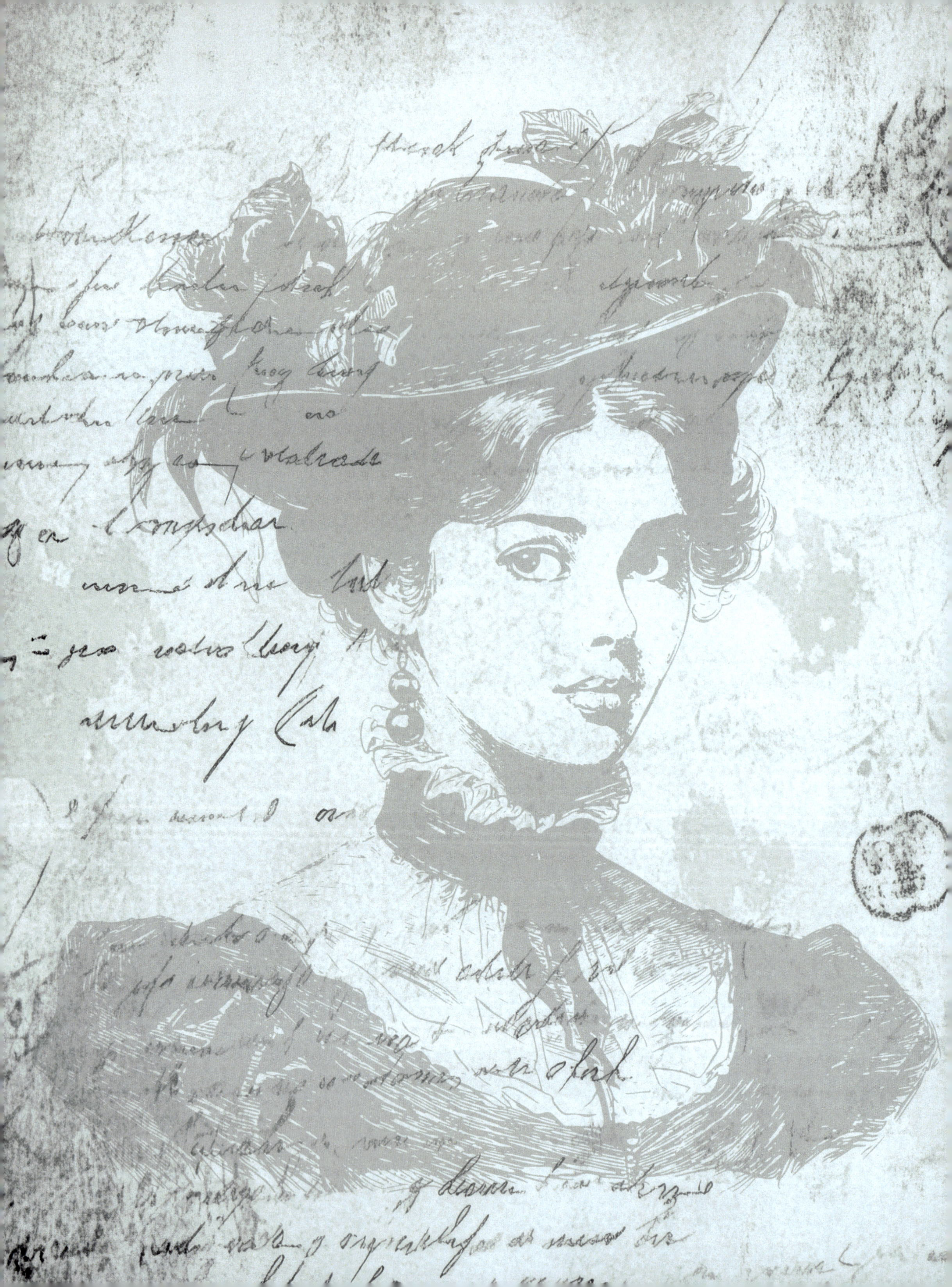

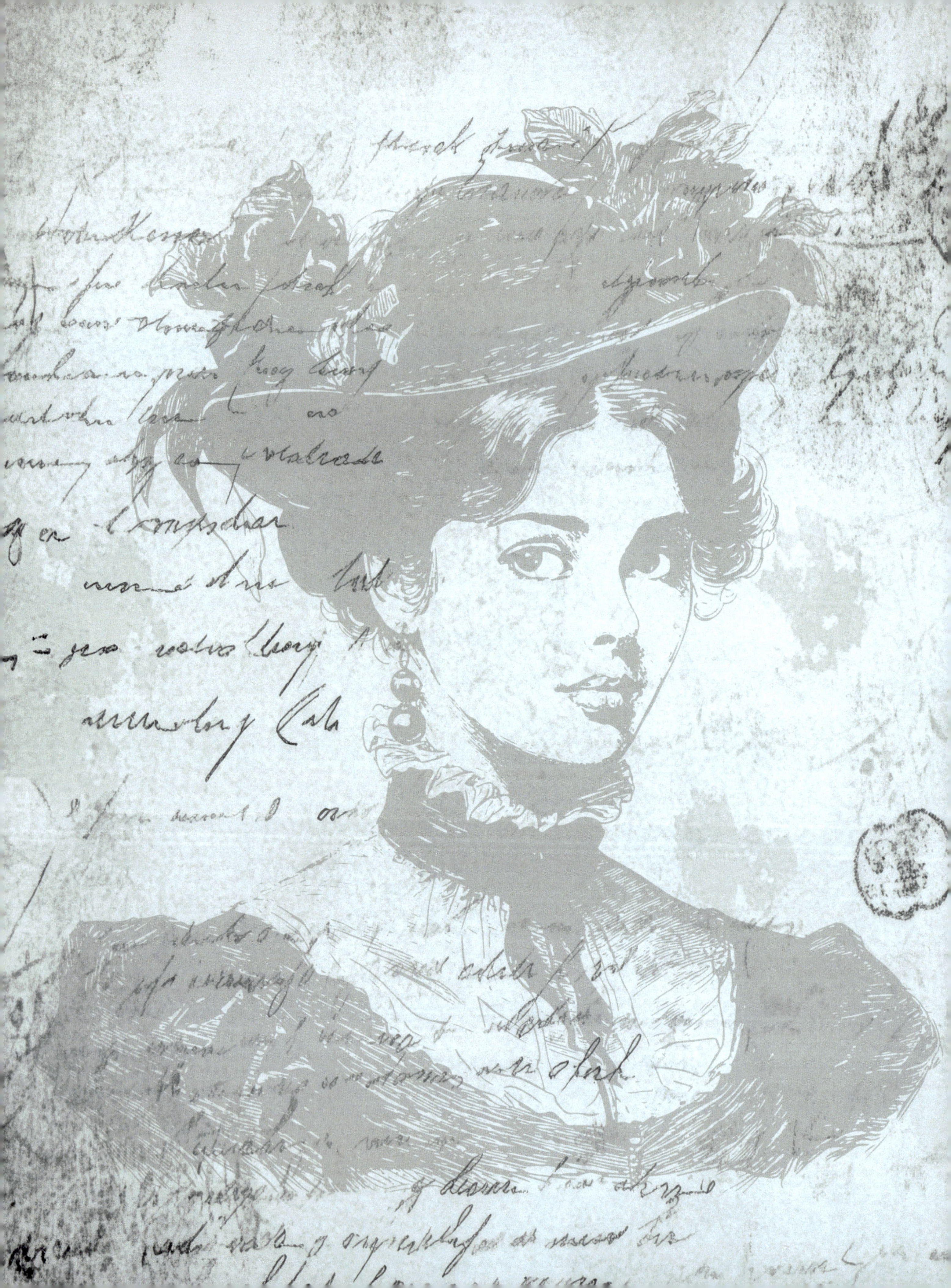

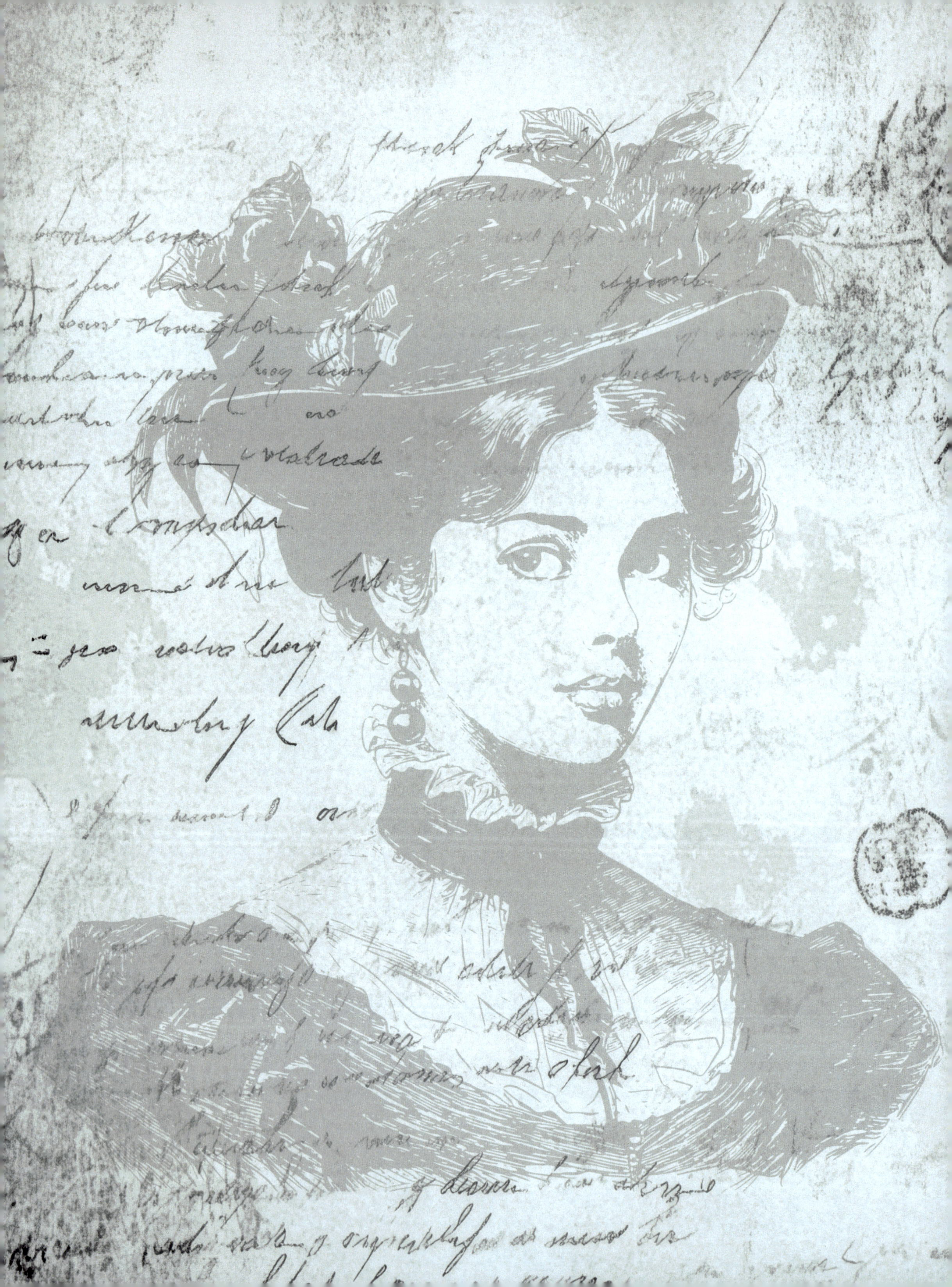

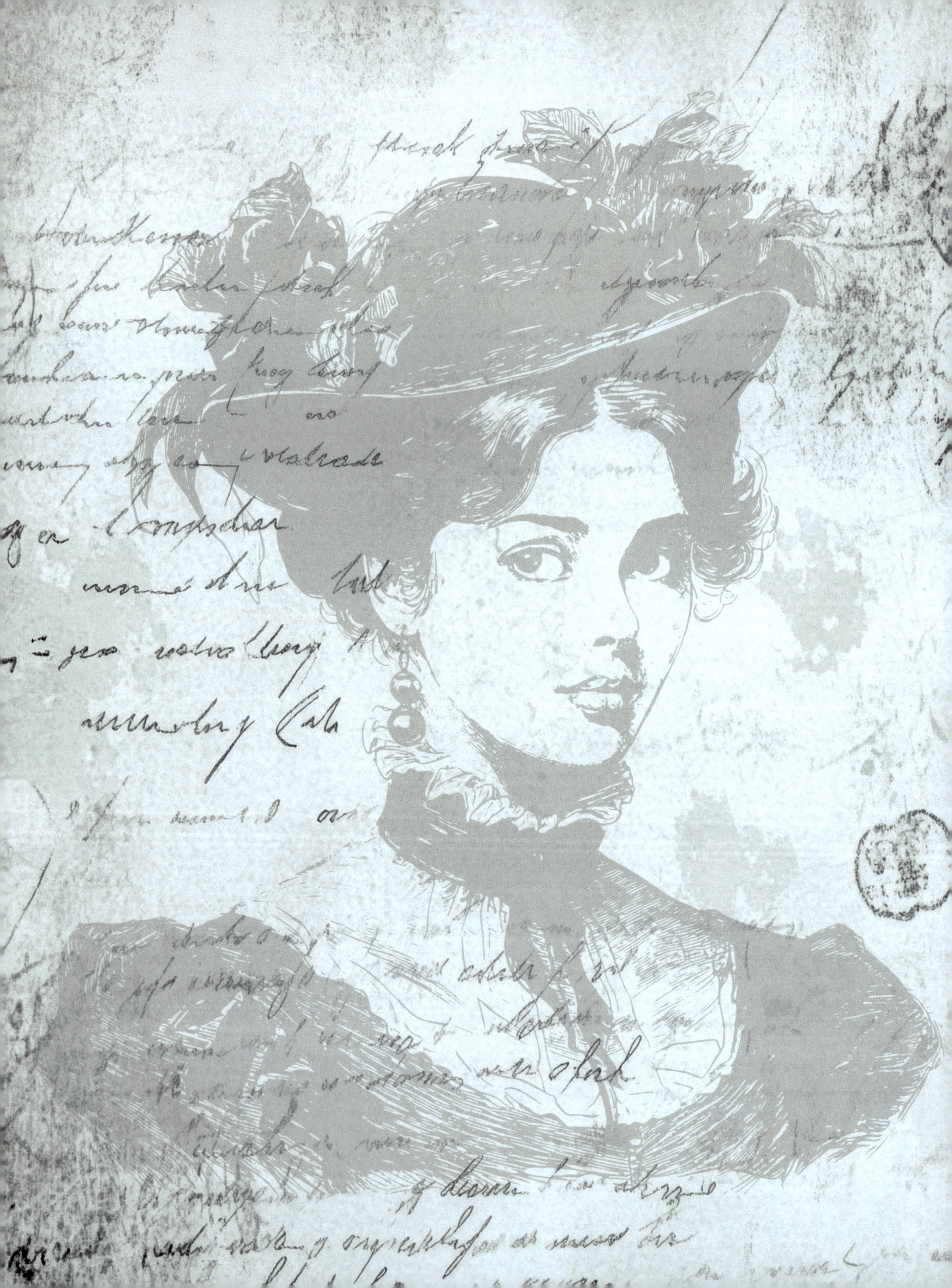

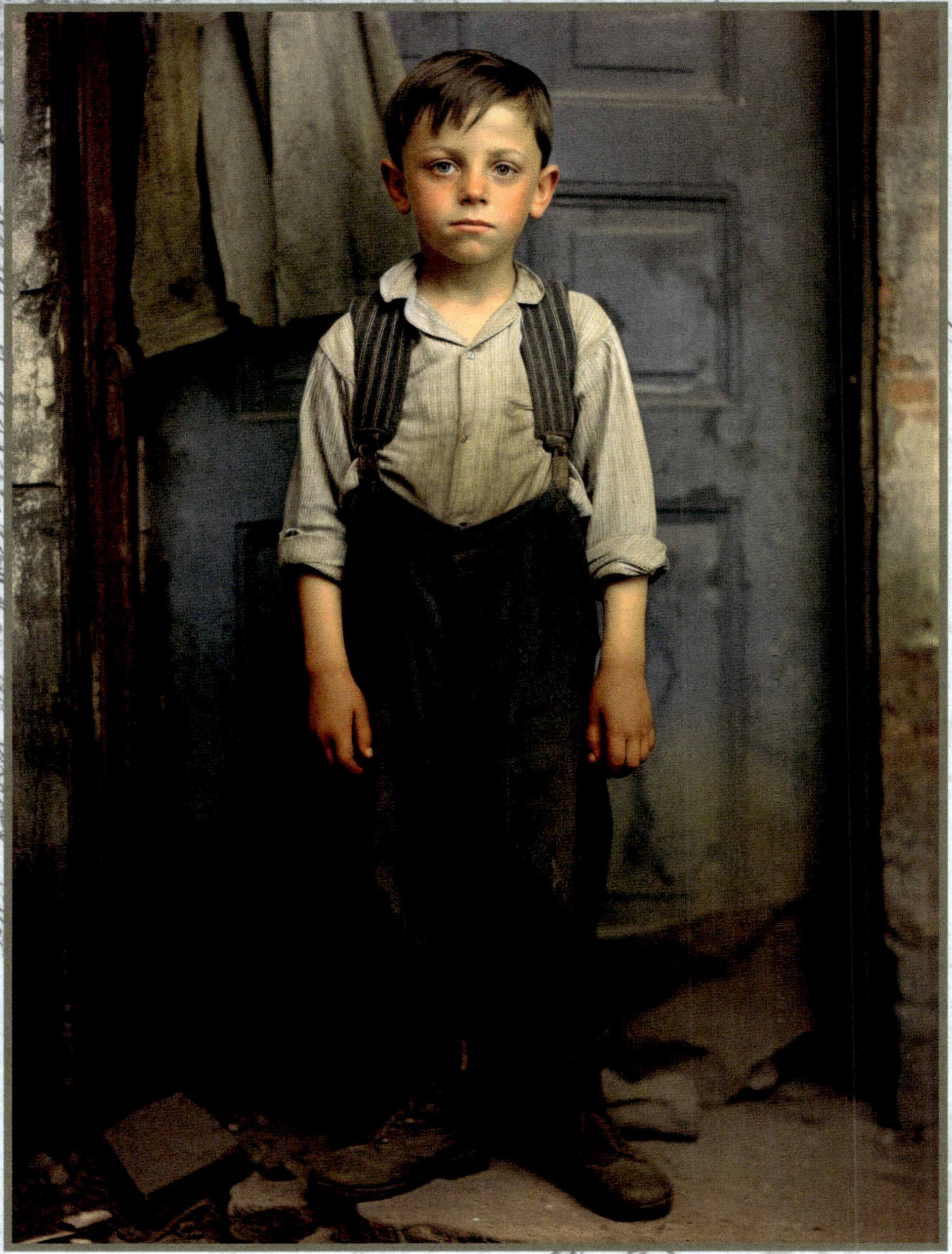

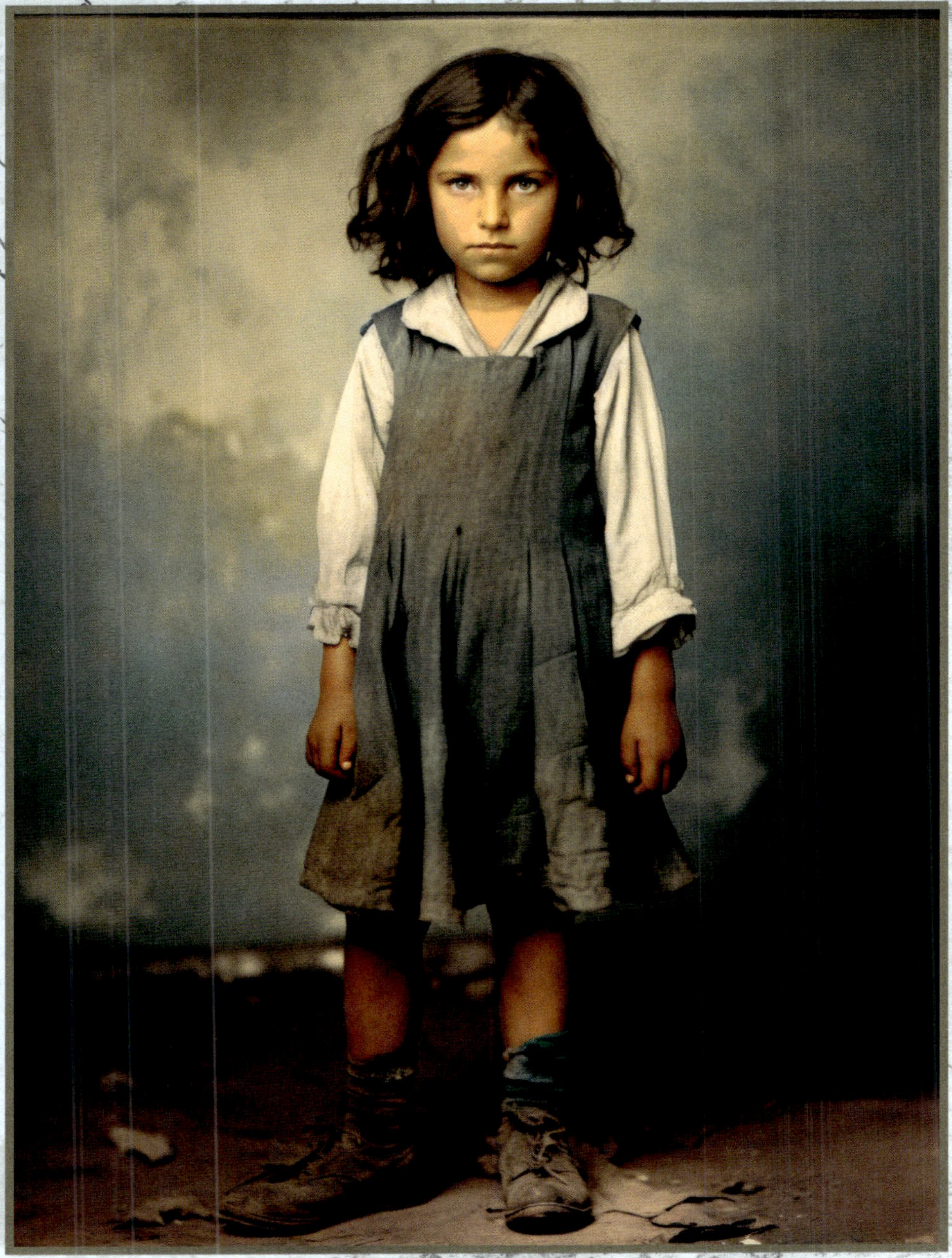

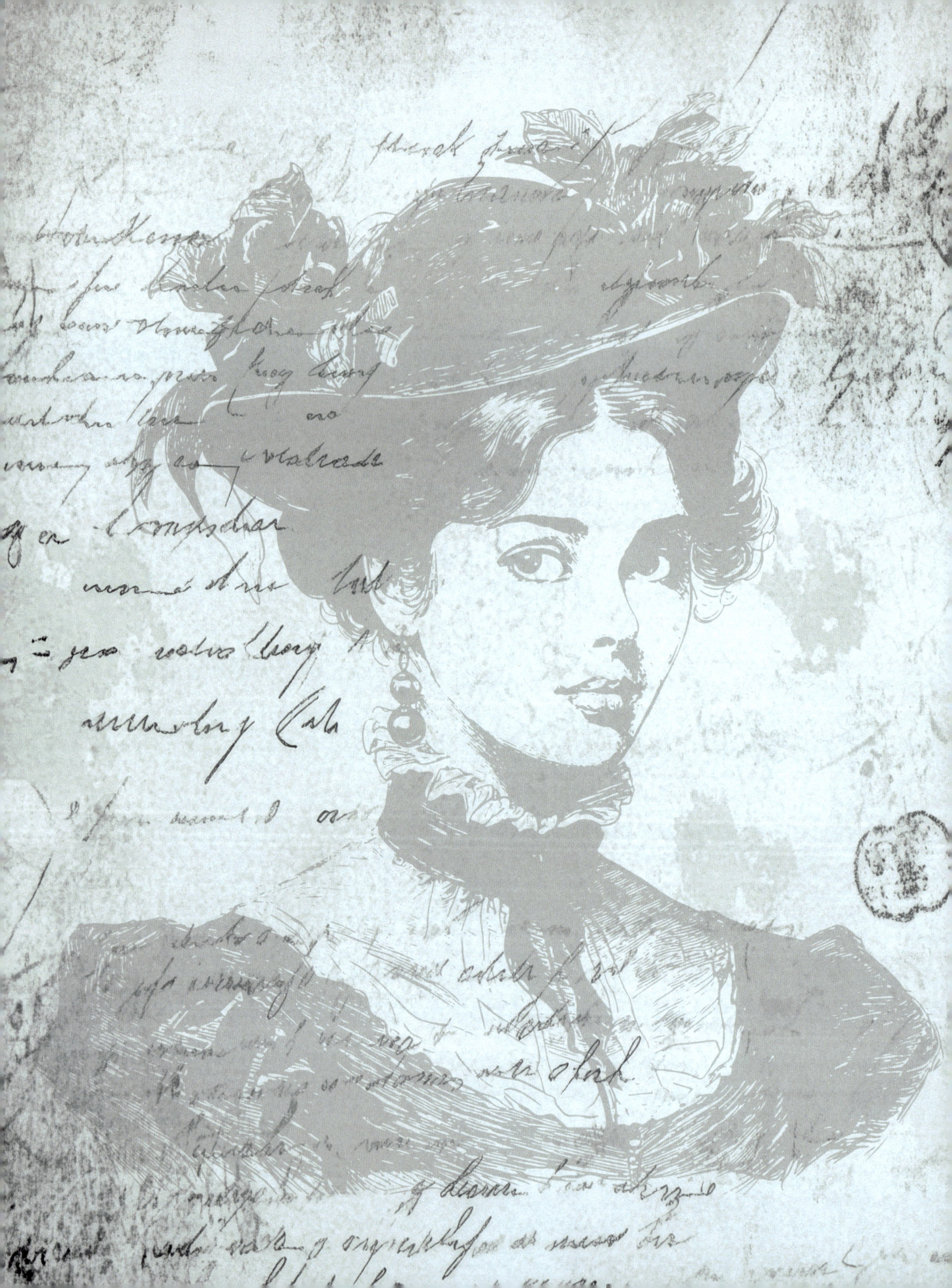

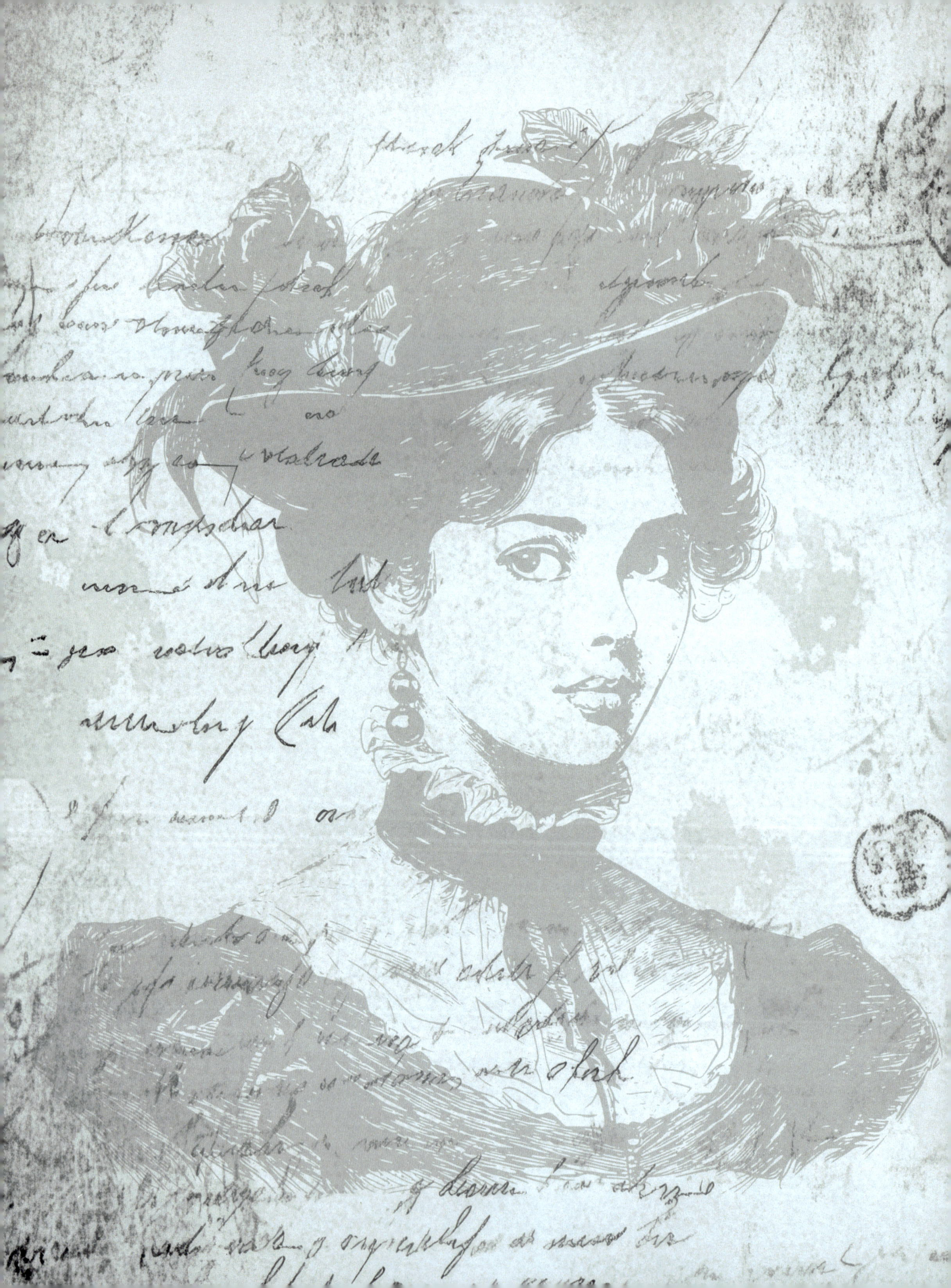

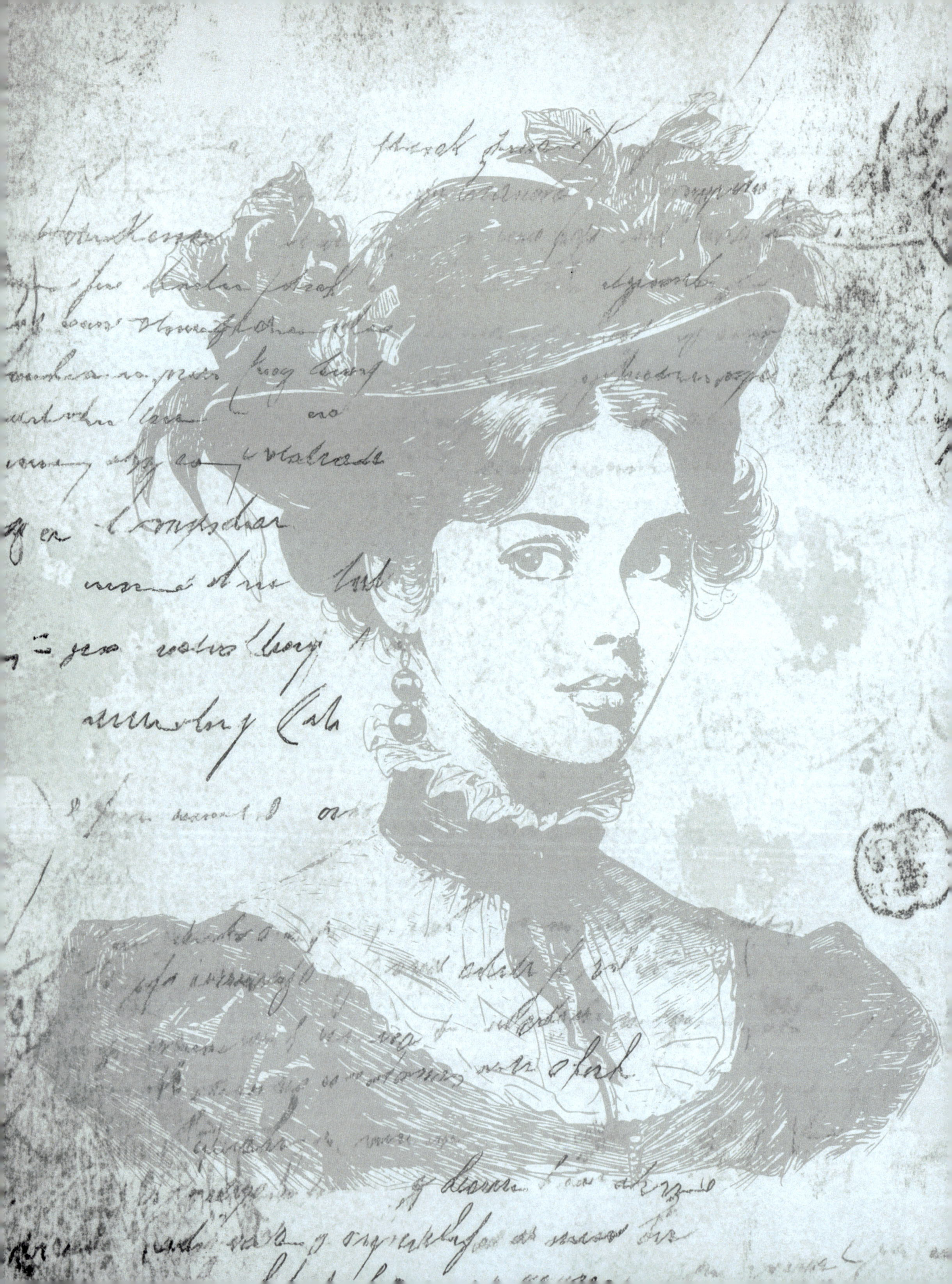

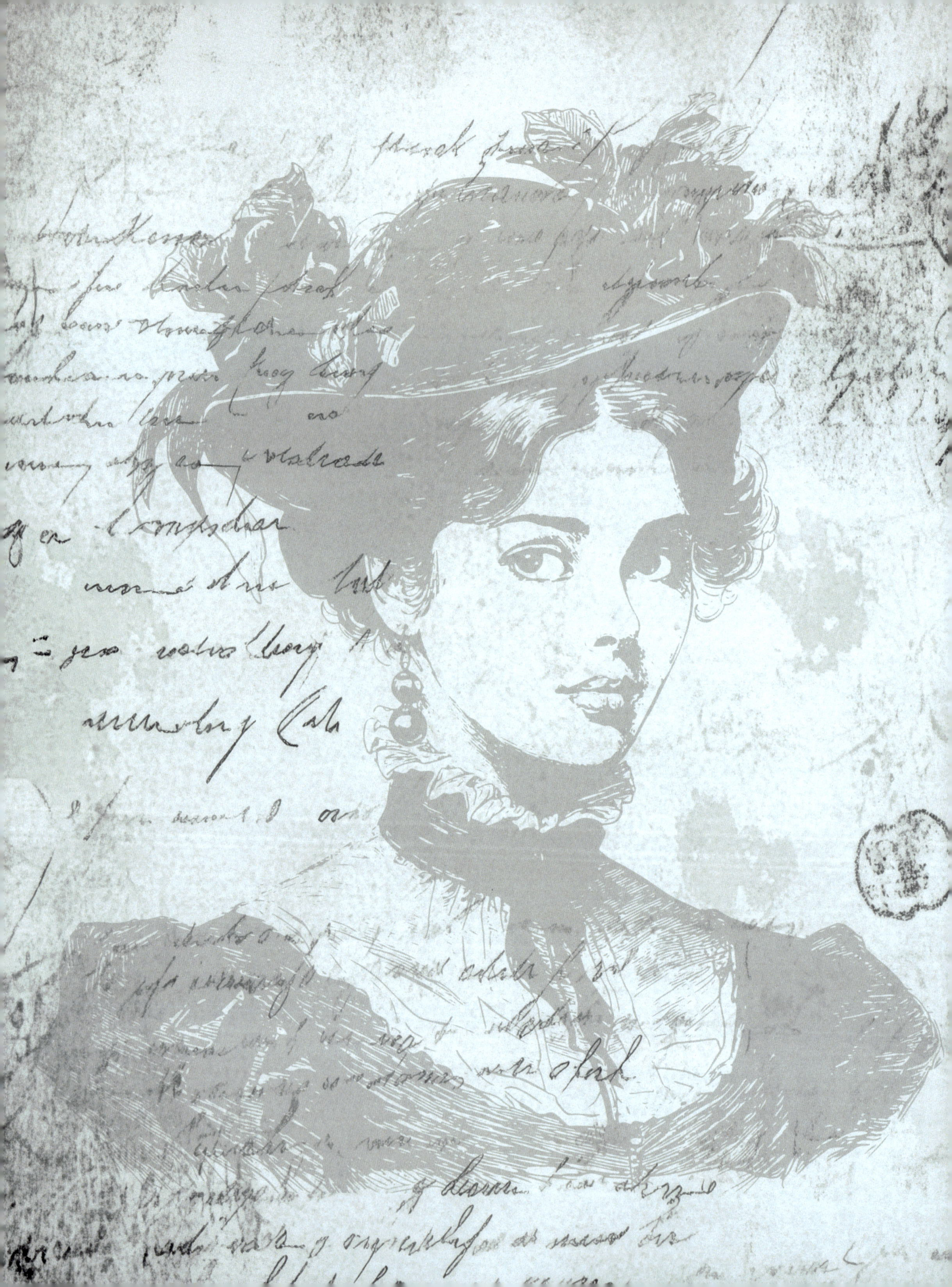

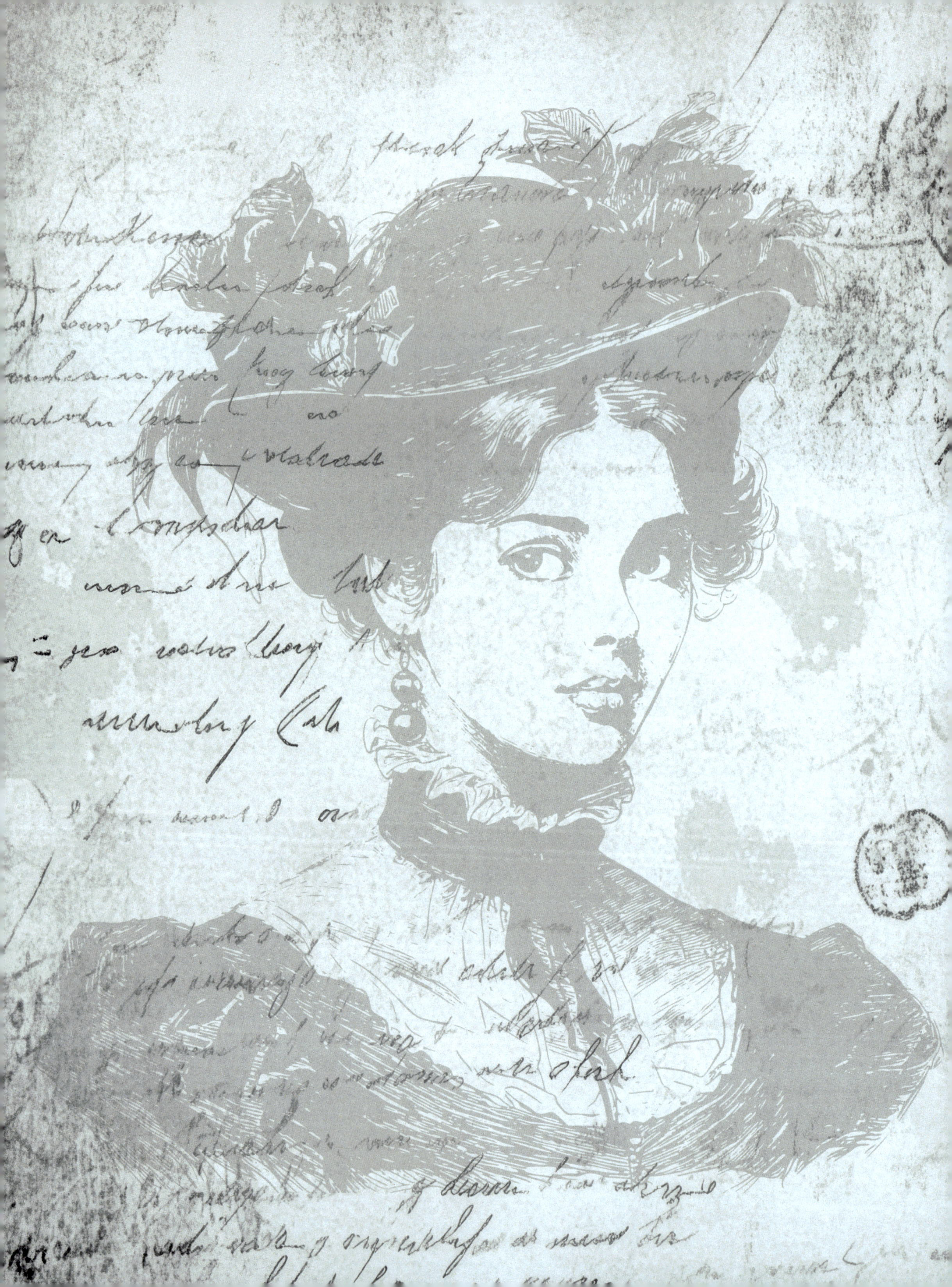

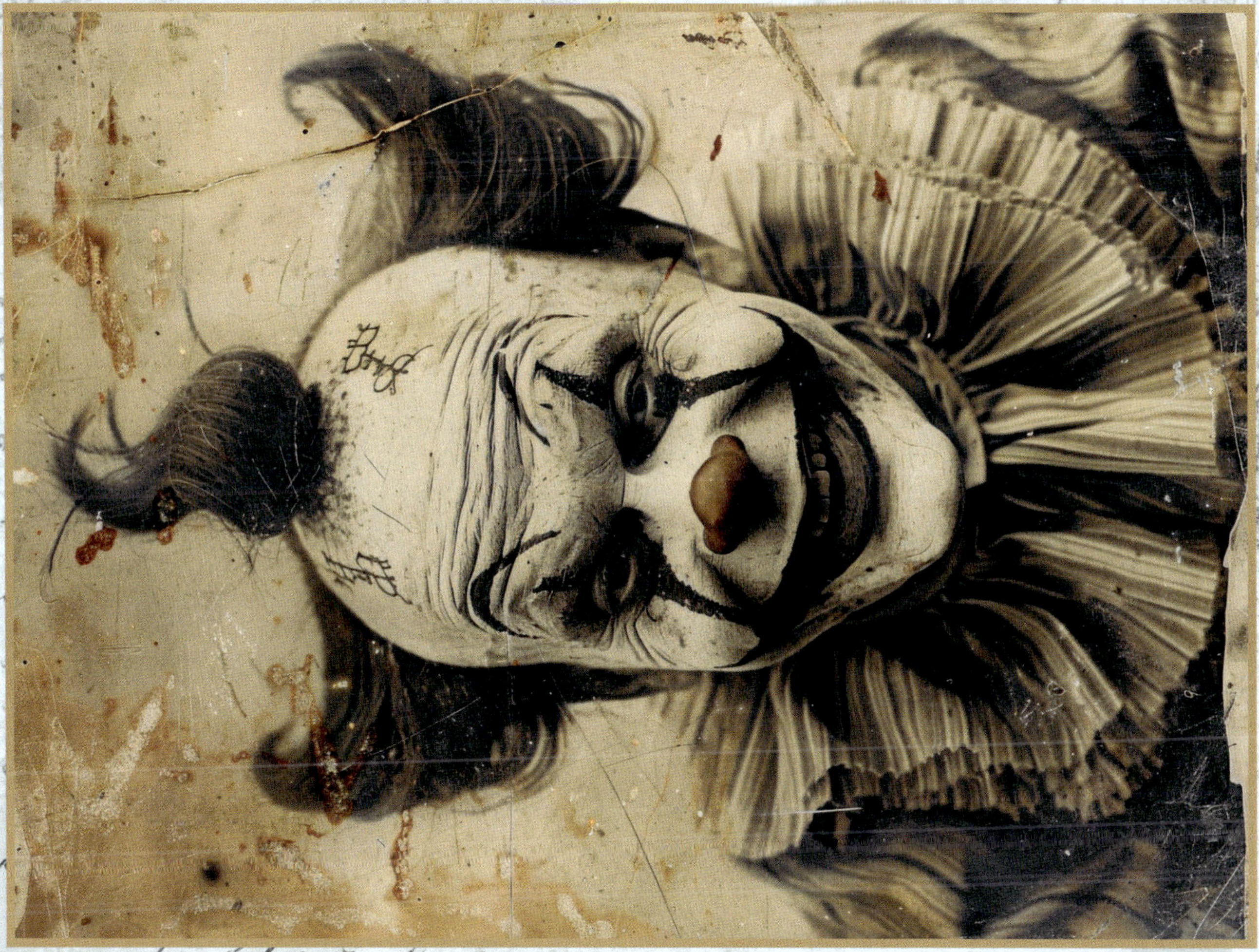

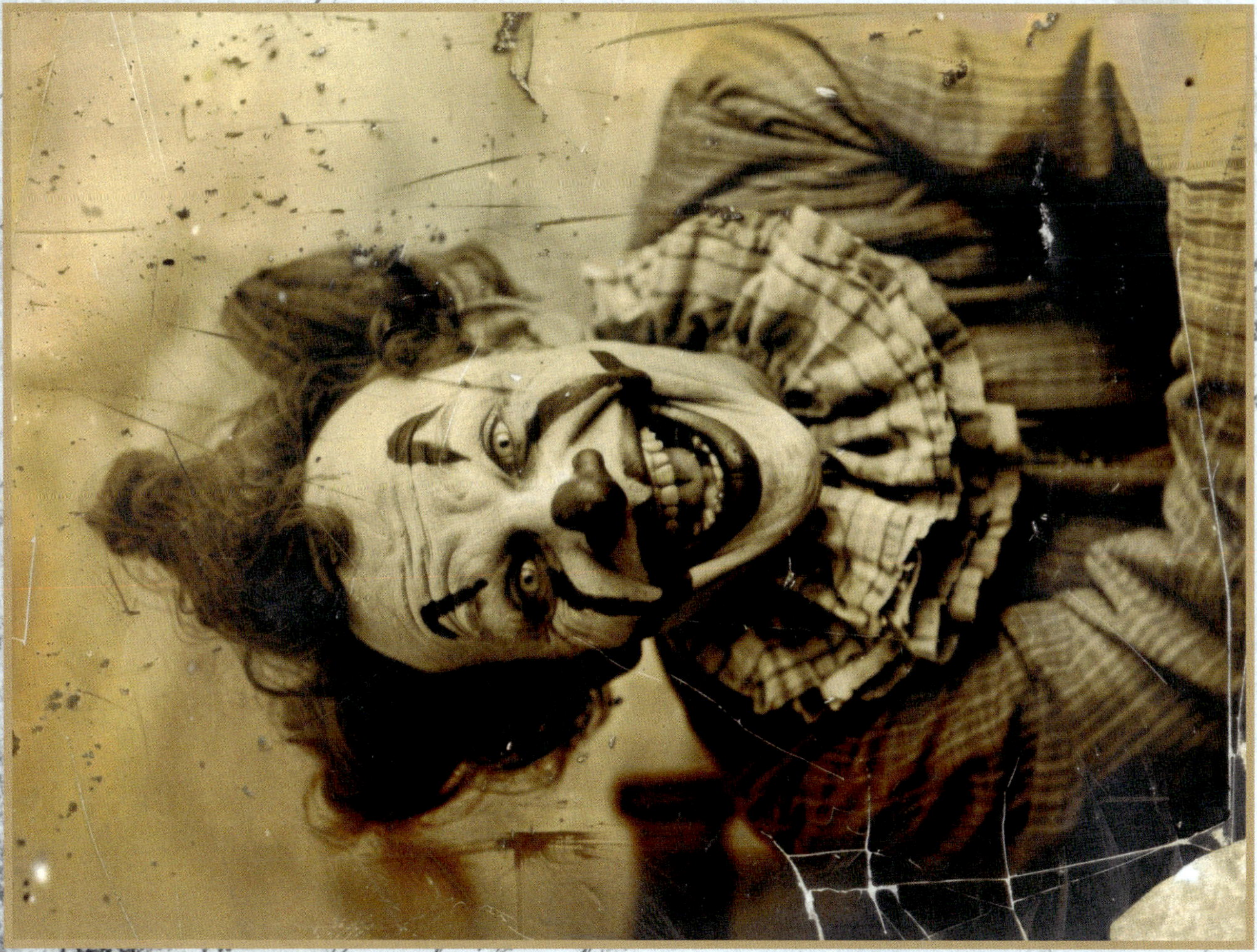

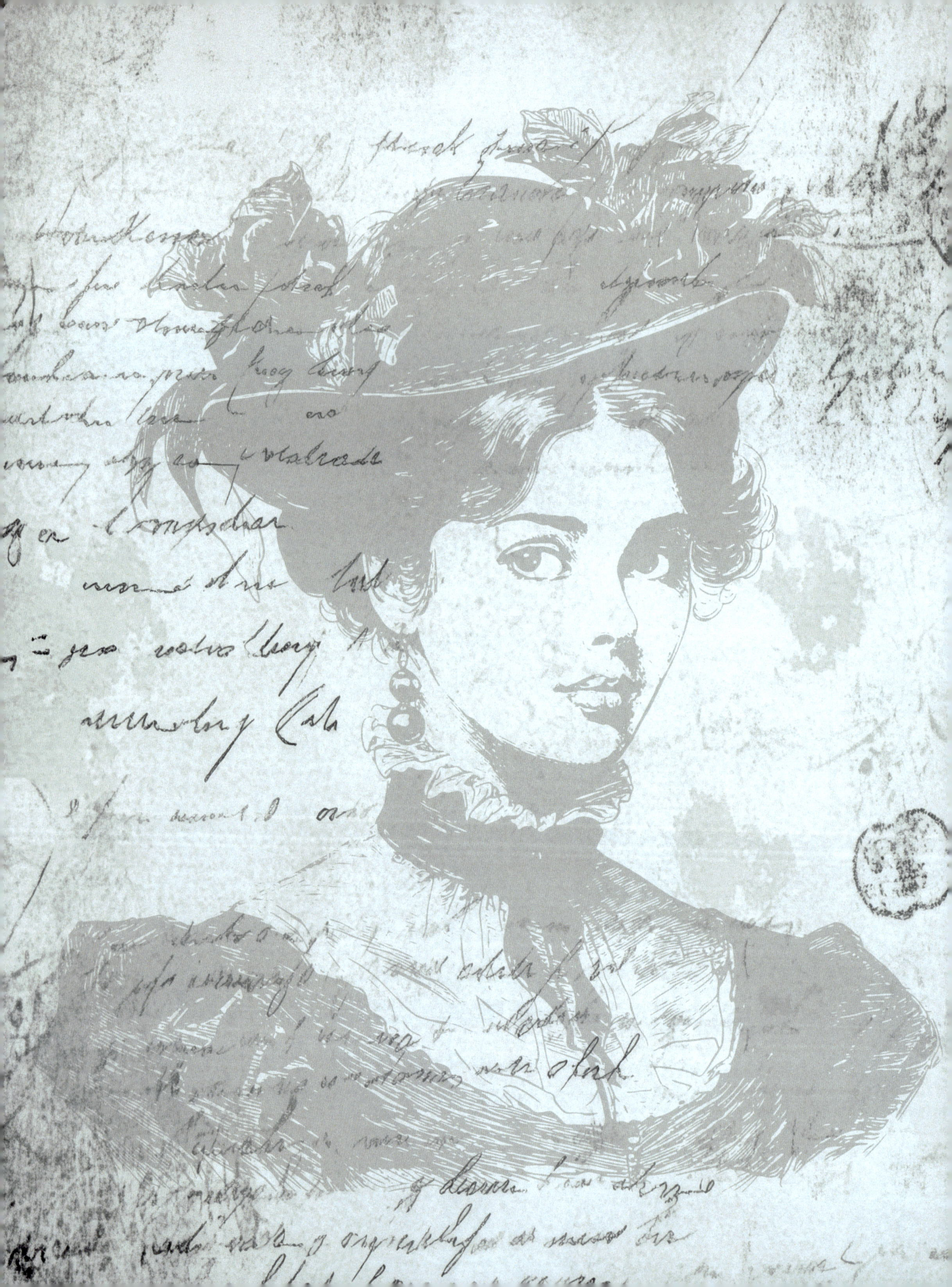

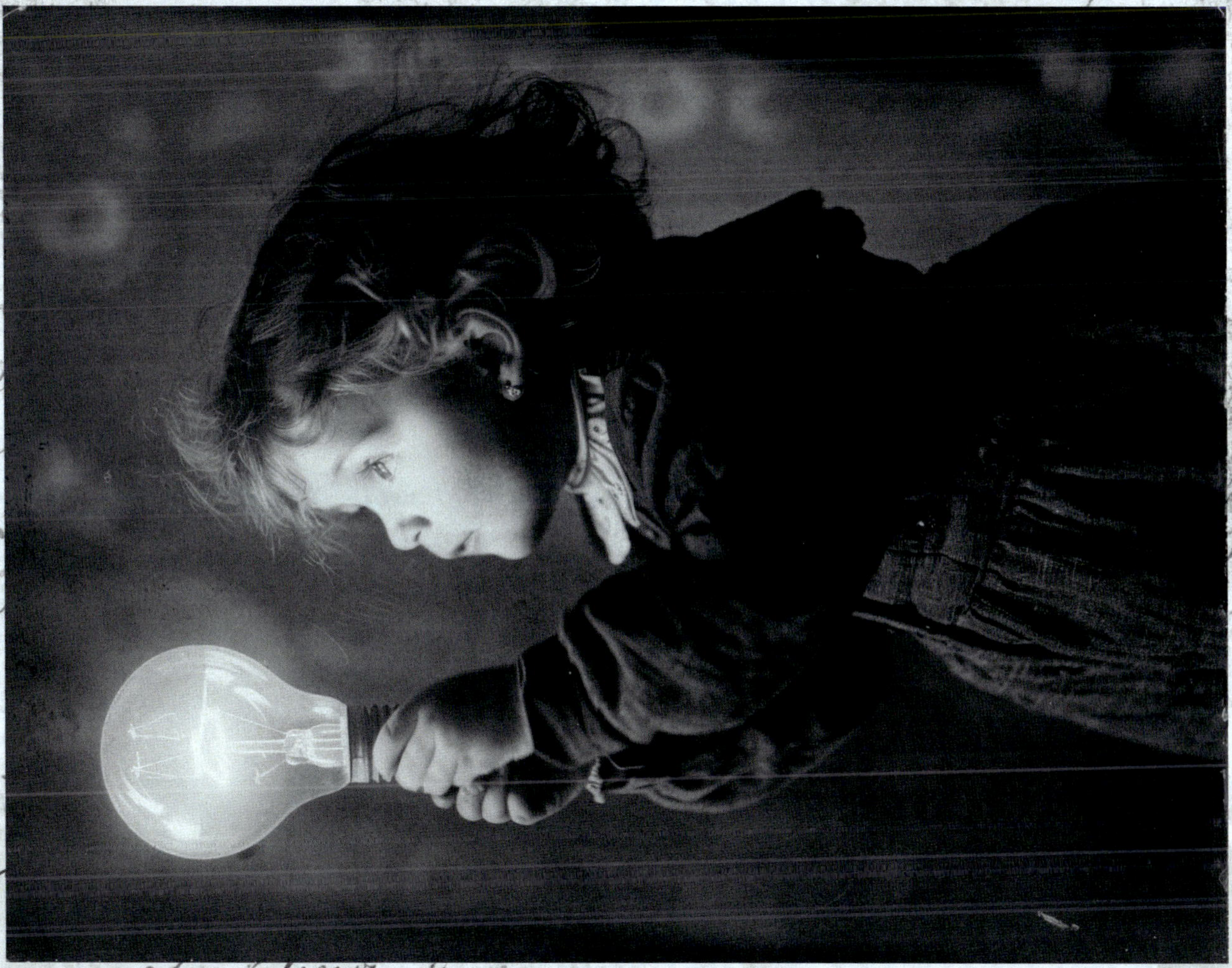

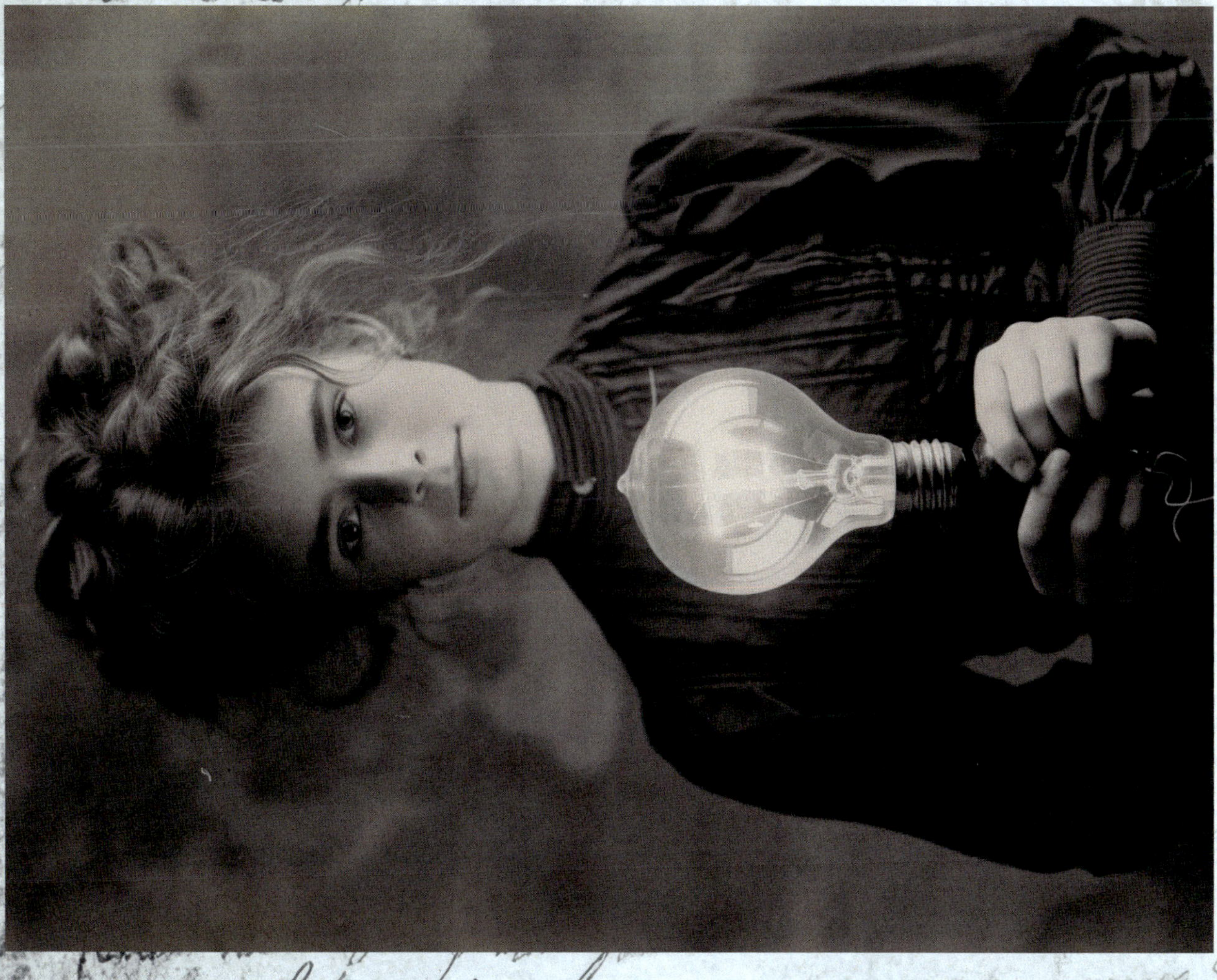

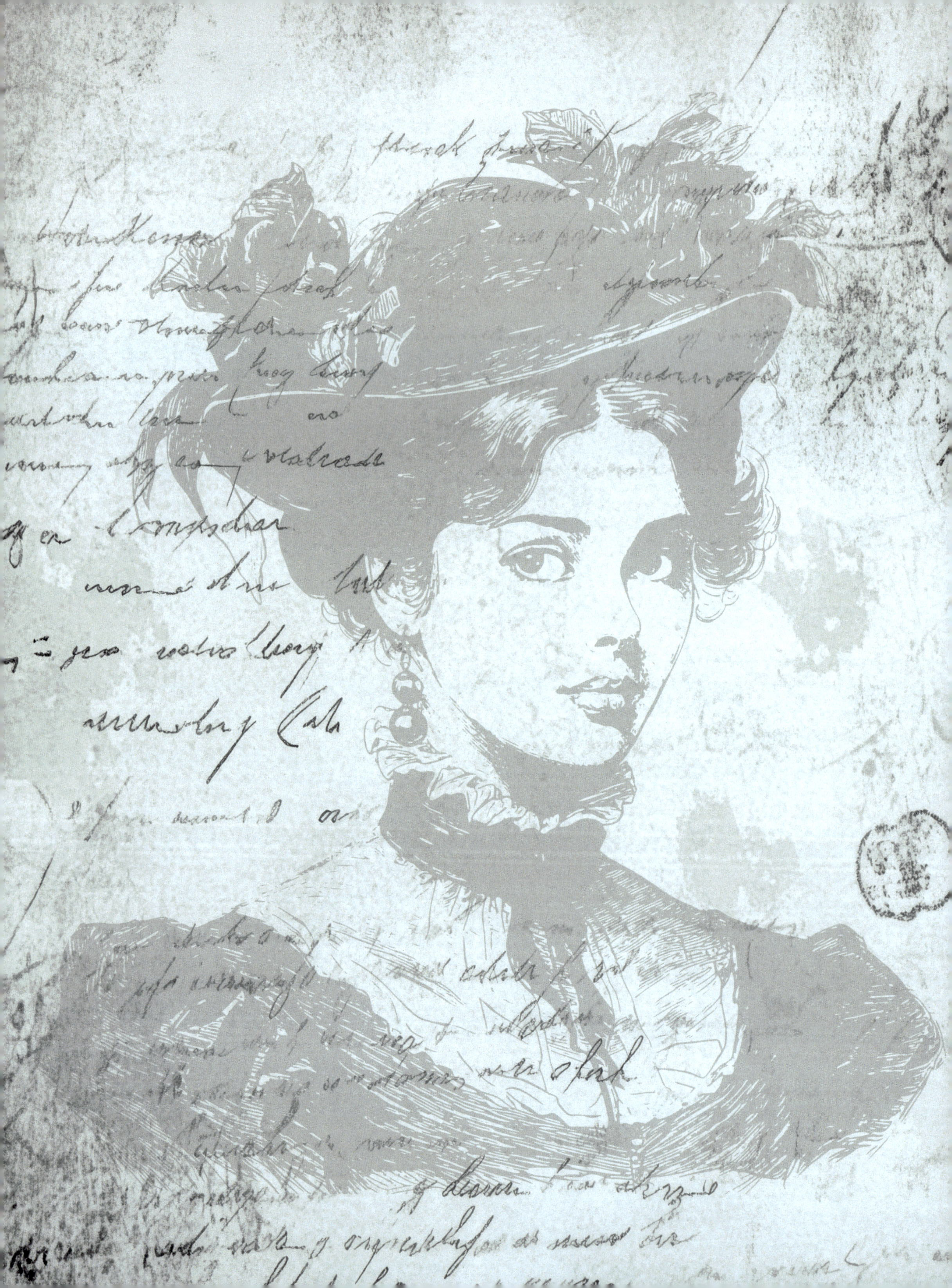

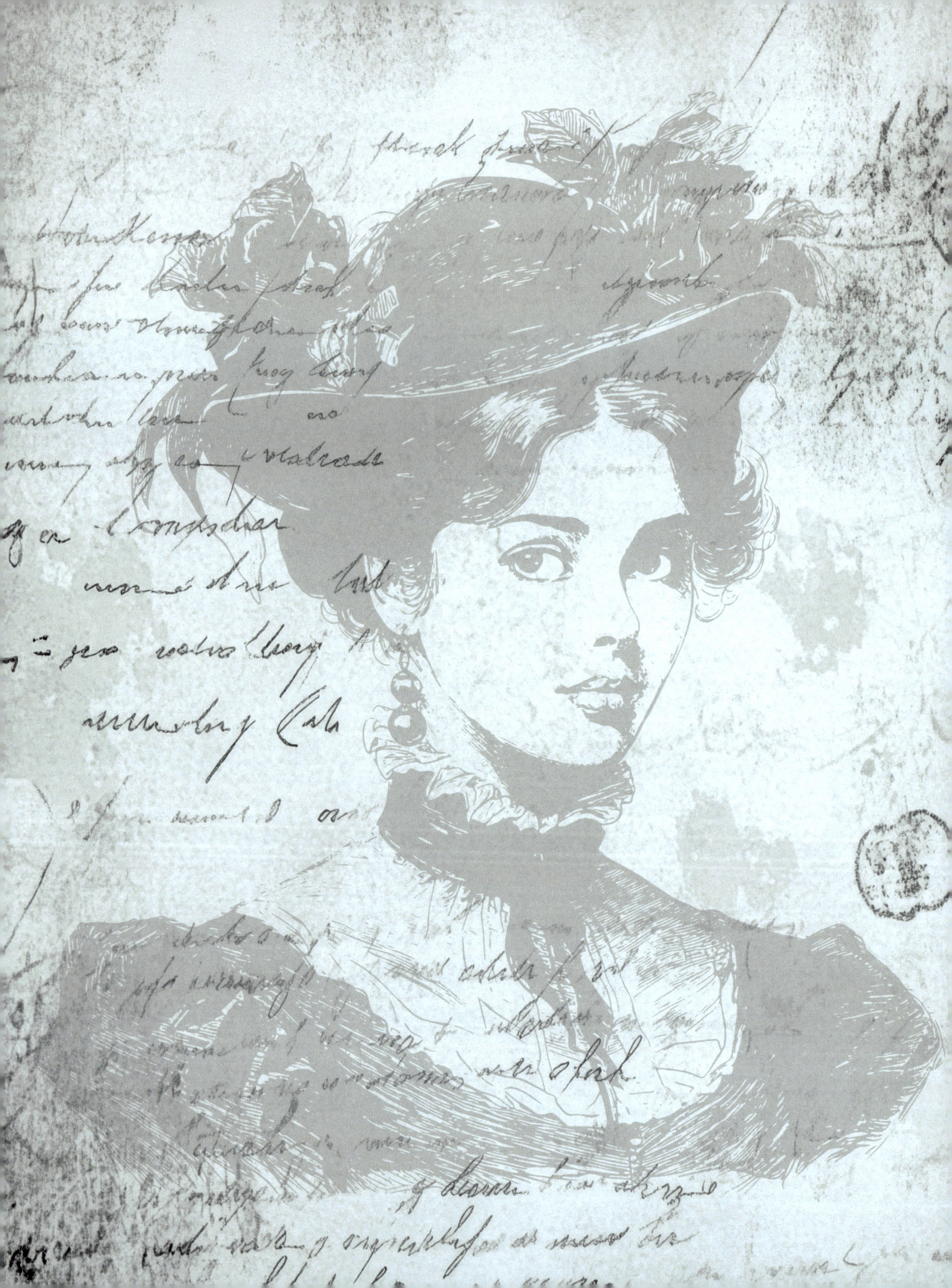

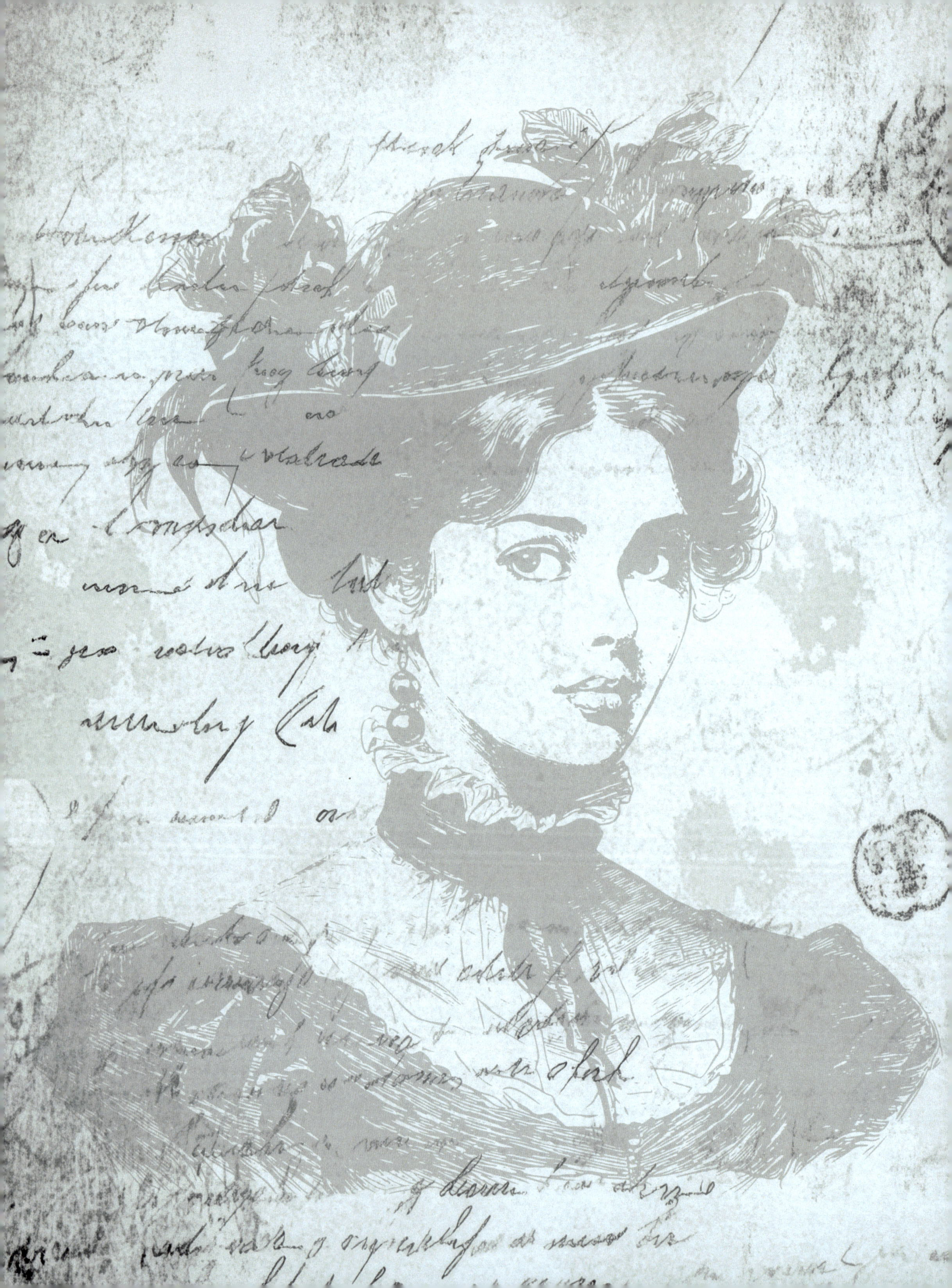

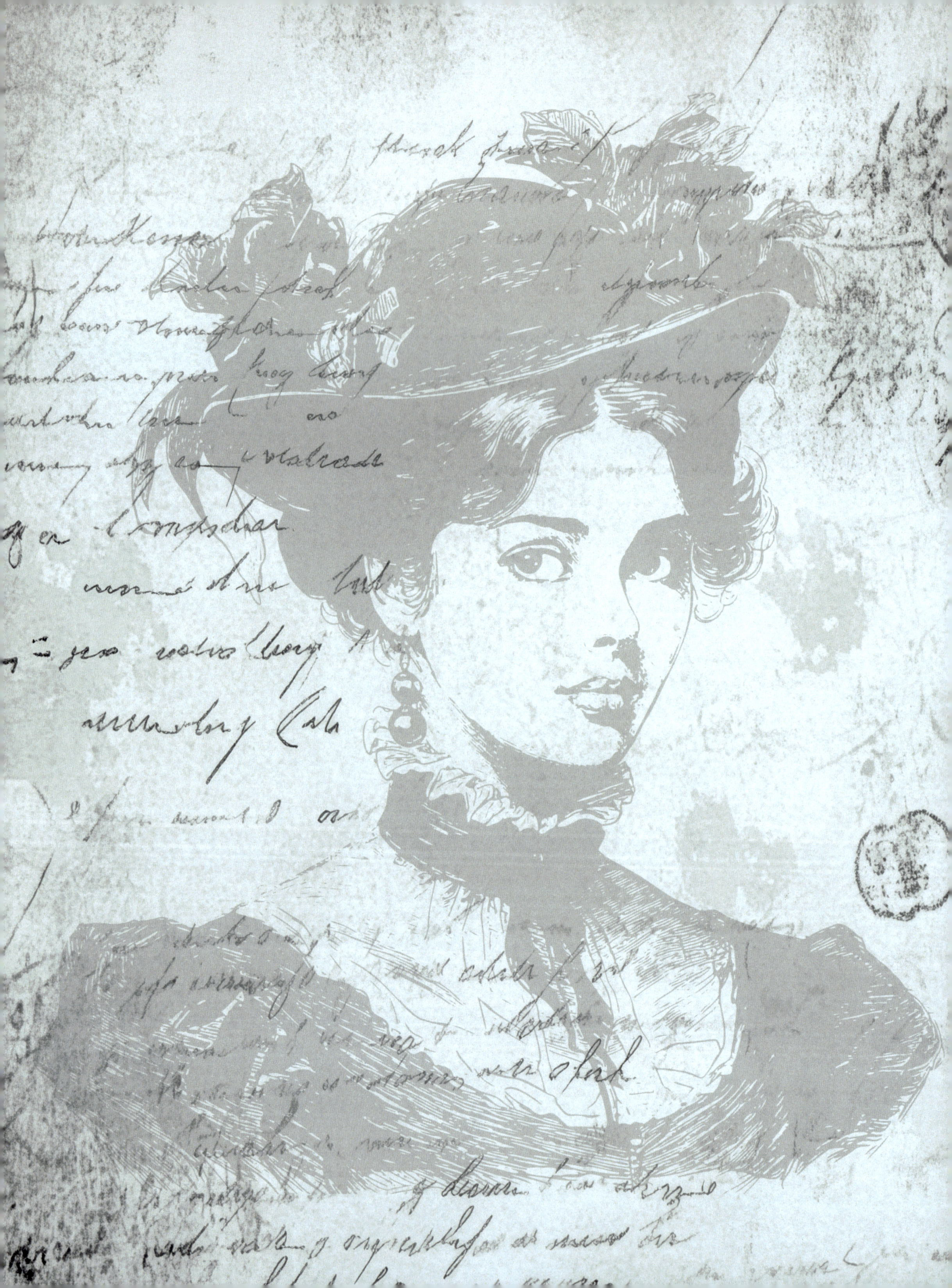

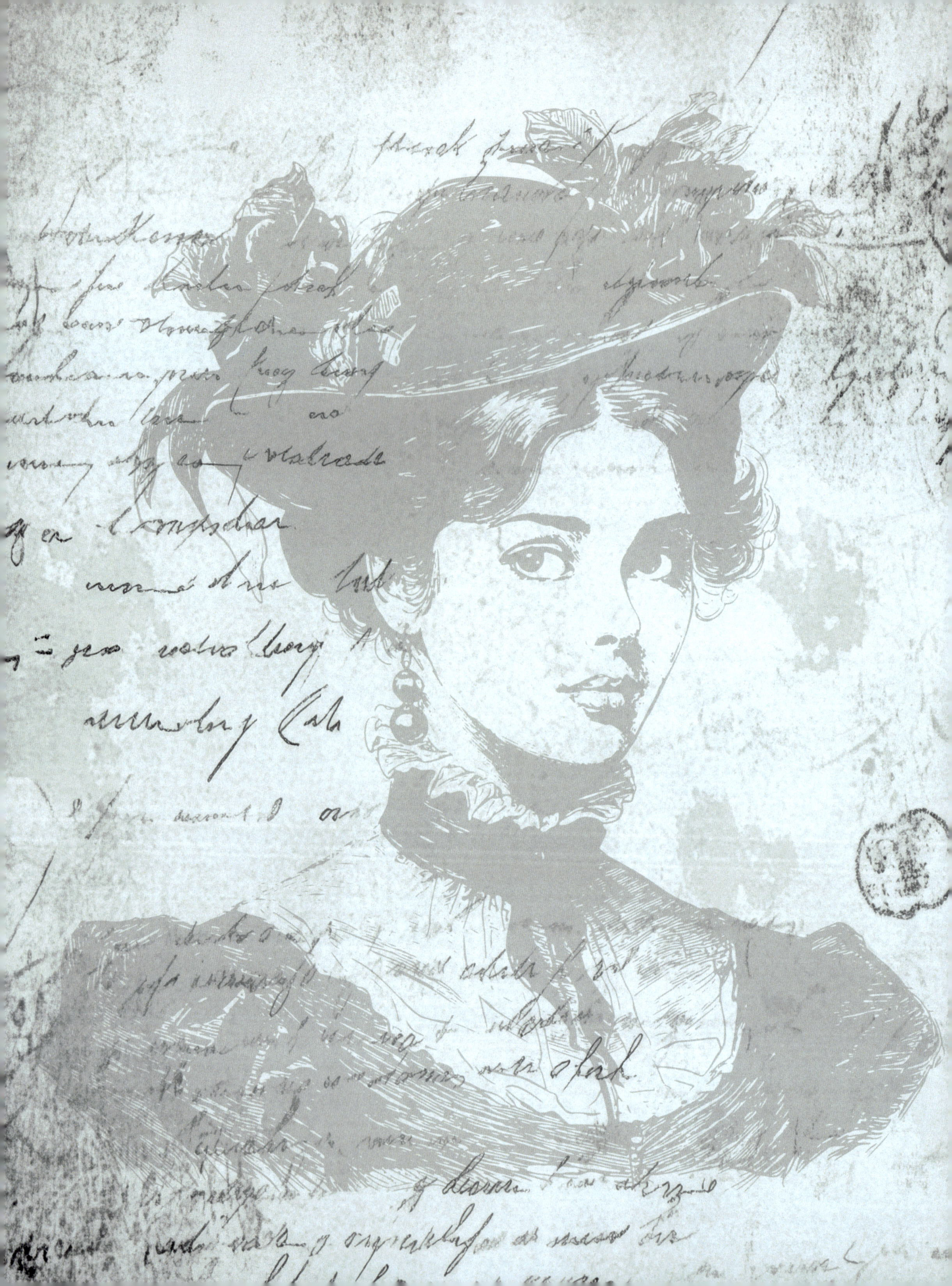

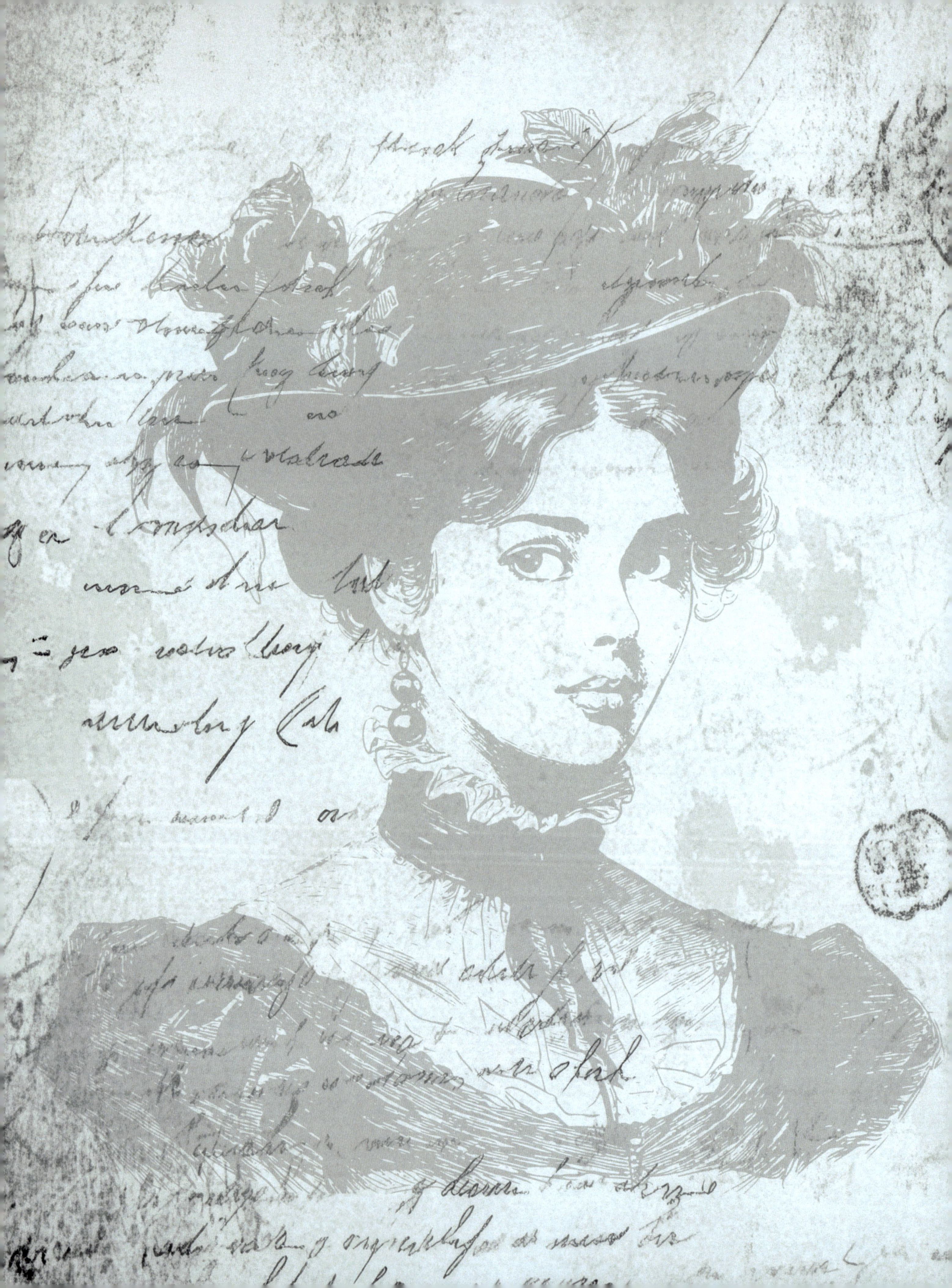

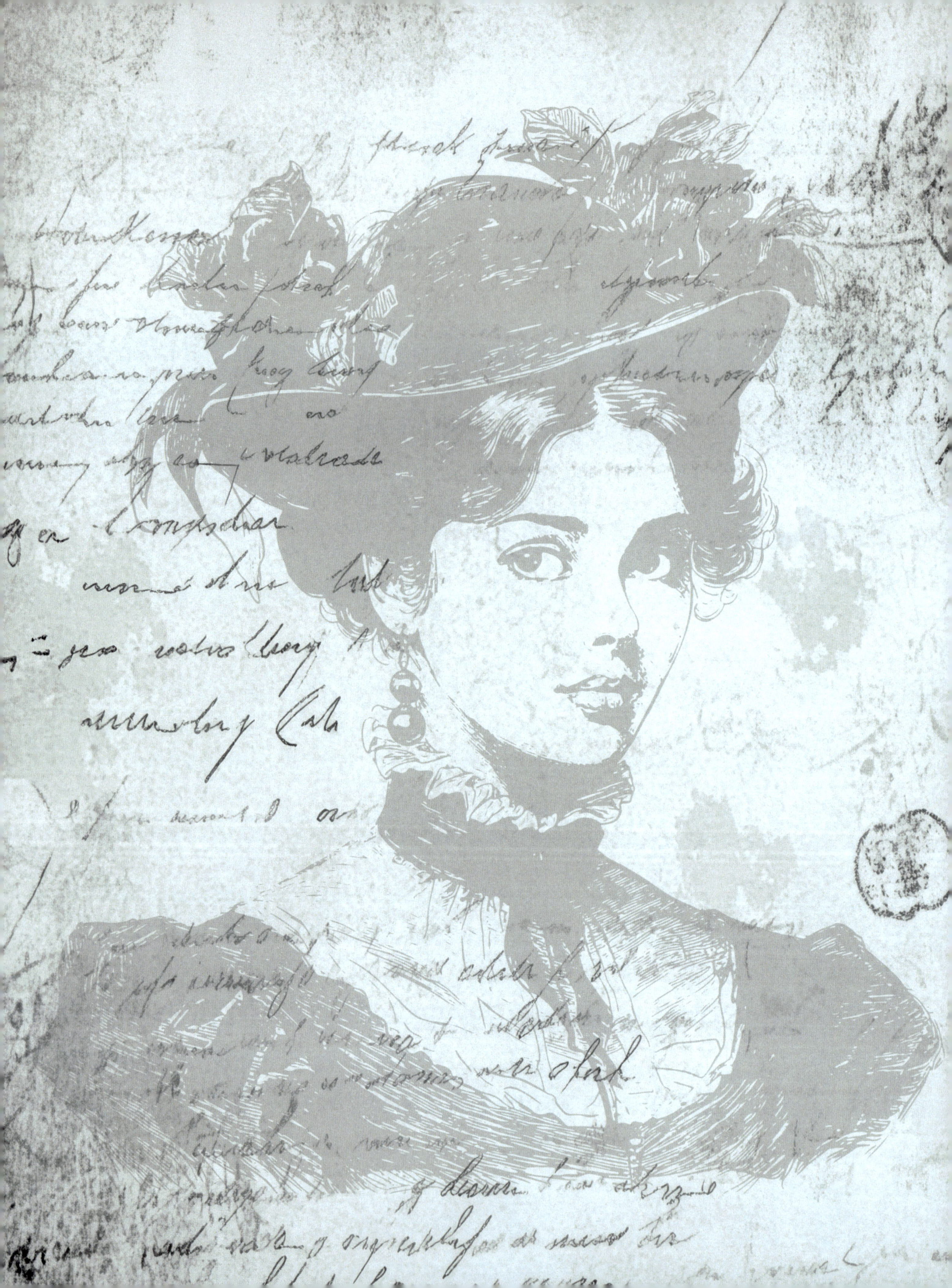

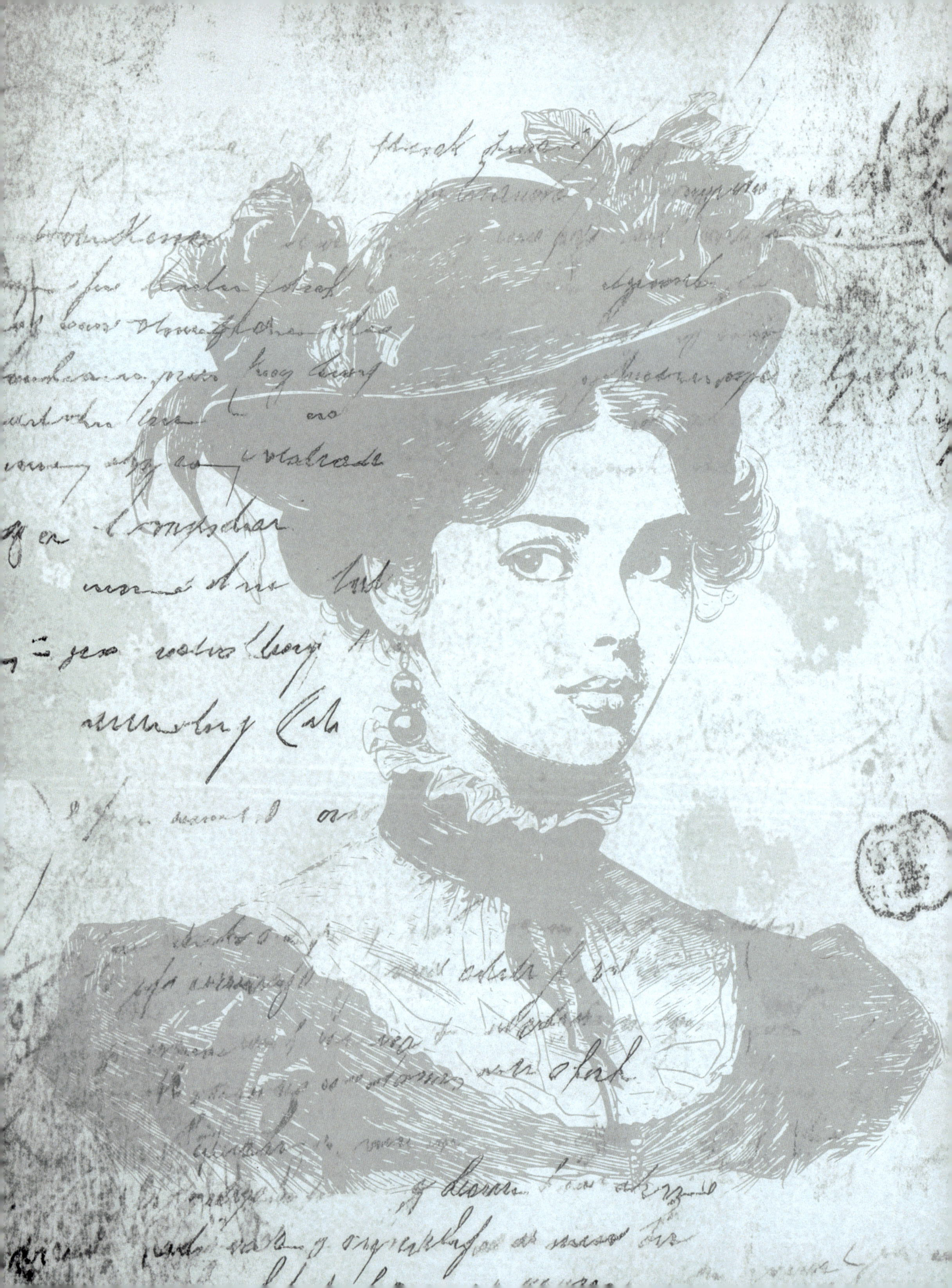

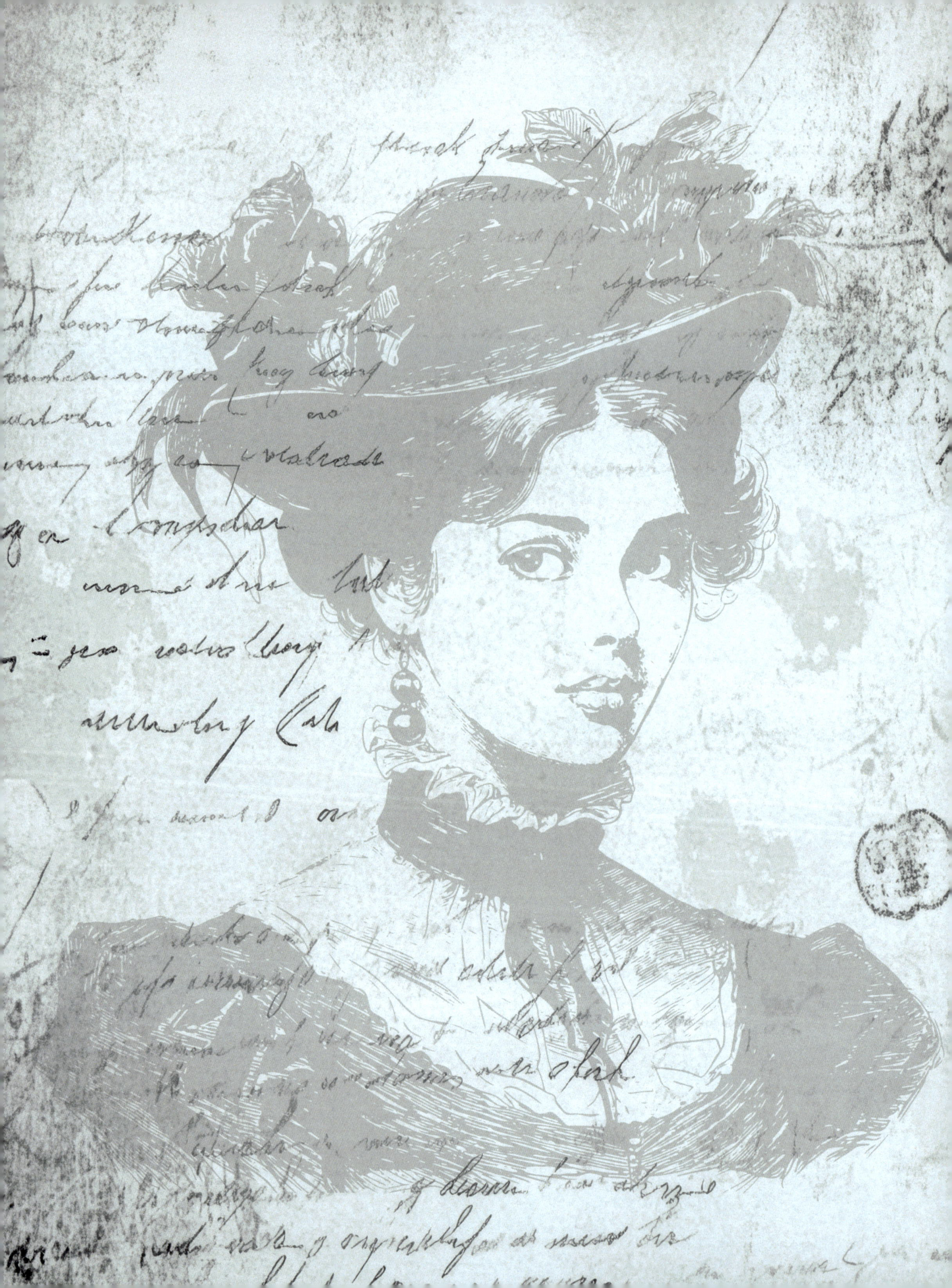

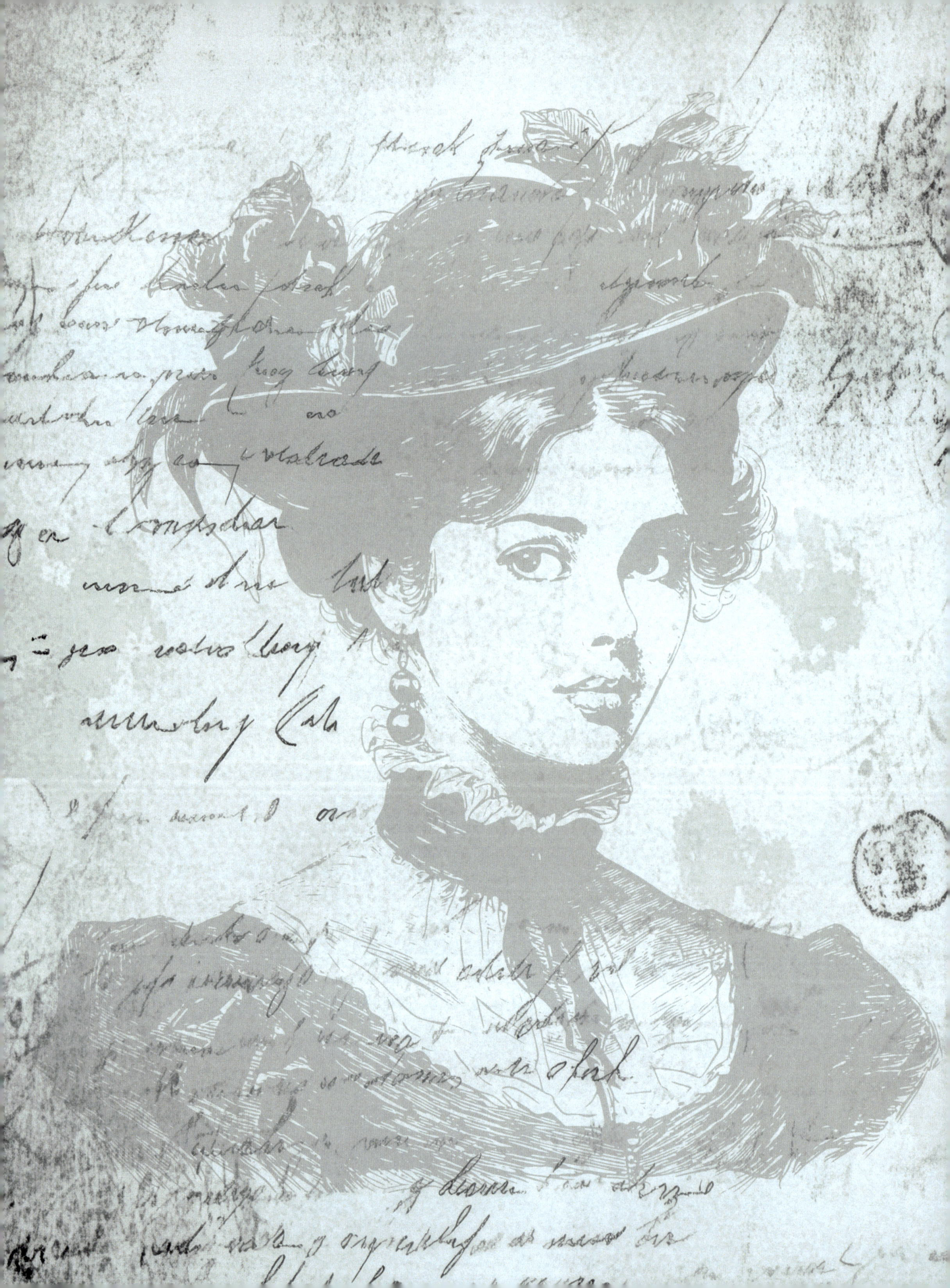

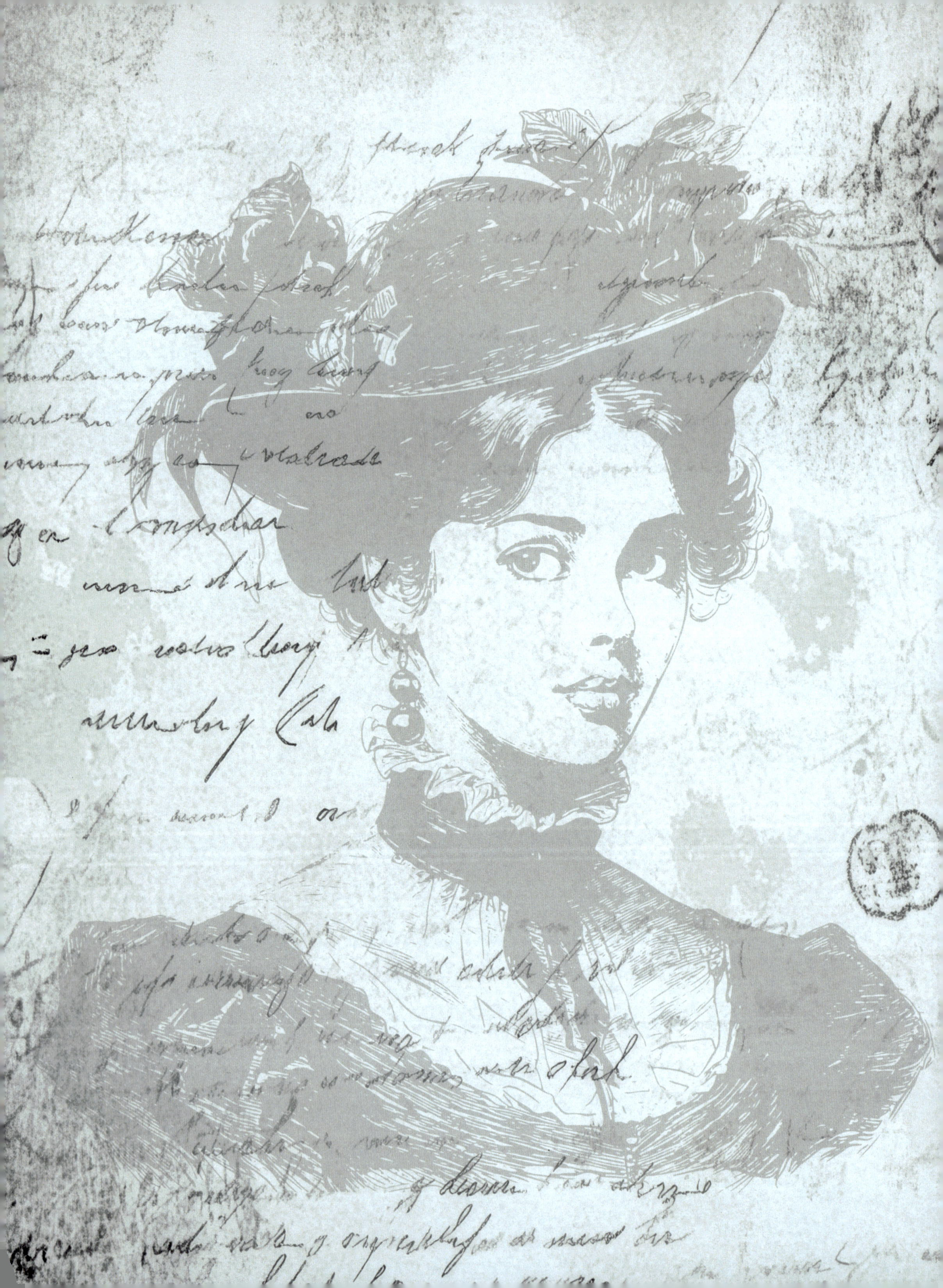

UNLOCK YOUR EXCLUSIVE
BONUS DIGITAL PACK!

This book comes with a bonus digital pack, packed with additional images and backgrounds to enhance your experience.

How to Access Your Digital Pack

Visit:
https://craftandcherish.com/vintage-faces-book
or scan the QR code below.

1. Scroll down to the '**Download Resources**' section and click on the '**Book's Digital Pack**' tab.

2. Click the '**Password-Protected Files**' button, fill out the form and click '**Download**' to receive a PDF with the Google Drive URL.

3. **Download the ZIP file** onto your computer. **Unzip it** on your computer by typing *craftandcherishvintagefaces* as the password.

We hope you enjoy these exclusive resources to enhance your creative journey!

MORE TITLES FROM
CRAFT AND CHERISH

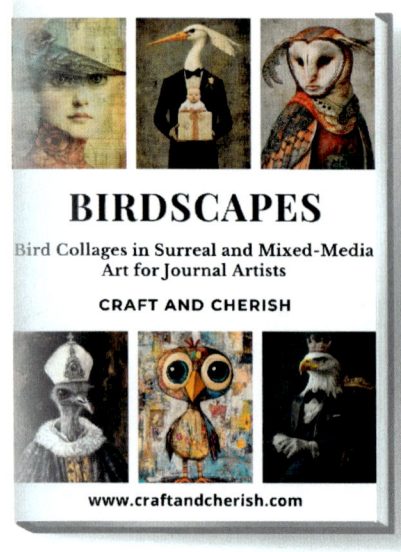
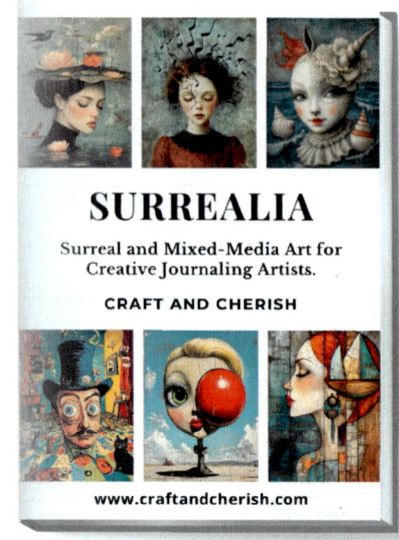

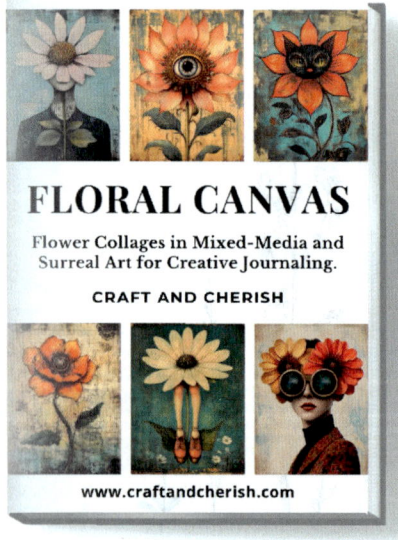
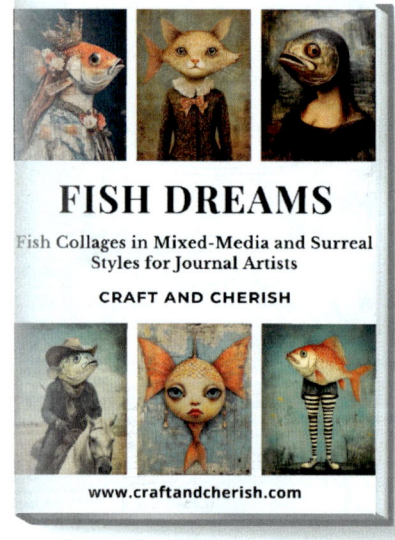

Scan the code or visit our website to see what's NEXT?

https://craftandcherish.com

Scan Me

Made in the USA
Monee, IL
25 February 2025

12942835R00064